POETIC WISDOM

Susan R. Makin, Ph.D., A.T.R.

Dr. Susan R. Makin is a registered art therapist and the author of *A Consumer's Guide to Art Therapy: For Prospective Employers, Clients and Students* (Thomas, 1994).

Using the arts for therapy, Susan works with groups and individuals from a variety of populations, consulting with the Toronto Hospital's Eating Disorders Programme as well as Canyon Ranch Health Resort's Behavorial Health Programme (Lenox, Massachusetts). She is also in private practice, and a mentor for many students writing dissertations.

A pioneer of poetry therapy techniques in Canada, Susan is an active member of the American organization, the National Association for Poetry Therapy. She is recognized for her creative journaling techniques integrating poetry, creative writing, and art-making.

Susan's Ph.D. is in Interdisciplinary Studies (Psychology, Sociology, Arts Therapies, and Health and Health Care). Born in Liverpool, England, she has lived in North America since 1981.

Peggy Osna Heller, Ph.D., R.P.T.

Dr. Peggy Osna Heller is a psychotherapist and clinical poetry therapist in private practice in Potomac, Maryland. She is the director of the poetry Therapy Training Institute and codirector of the Wordsworth Center for Growth and Healing.

Peggy has taught courses in poetry therapy at universities and colleges nationally. She is also an executive officer of the Bibliotherapy Round Table and a past president of the National Association for Poetry Therapy, and serves on the editorial boards of the journals of *Poetry Therapy* and *Arts in Psychotherapy*, respectively.

POETIC WISDOM
Revealing and Healing

By

Susan R. Makin, Ph.D.

With a Foreword by

Peggy Osna Heller, Ph.D.

CHARLES C THOMAS • PUBLISHER, LTD.
Springfield • Illinois • U.S.A.

Published and Distributed Throughout the World by

CHARLES C THOMAS • PUBLISHER, LTD.
2600 South First Street
Springfield, Illinois 62794-9265

© *1998 by* CHARLES C THOMAS • PUBLISHER, LTD.
ISBN 0-398-06878-X (cloth)
ISBN 0-398-06879-8 (paper)

Library of Congress Catalog Card Number:98-16987

With THOMAS BOOKS *careful attention is given to all details of manufacturing and design. It is the Publisher's desire to present books that are satisfactory as to their physical qualities and artistic possibilities and appropriate for their particular use.* THOMAS BOOKS *will be true to those laws of quality that assure a good name and good will.*

Printed in the United States of America
CR-R-3

Library of Congress Cataloging in Publication Data

Makin, Susan R.
    Poetic wisdom : revealing and healing / by Susan R. Makin ;
with a foreword by Peggy Osna Heller.
        p.   cm.
    Includes bibliographical references (p.).
    ISBN (invalid) 0-398-06808-X (cloth). -- ISBN 0-398-06879-8 (pbk.)
    1. Poetry--Therapeutic use.   I. Title.
RC489.P6M34   1998
615.8'515--dc21   98-16987
                                                                CIP

To
Dr. Arthur Lerner,
a founding father of poetry therapy,
who I had just begun to know.

Thanks

To Lev, my canine companion, for all her animal wisdom and love
To Shirley Makin, my mother, for all her moral support and
    encouragement
To Dr. Peggy Osna Heller, for her incredible mentorship and friendship
To Dr. George Olshin, for recognizing and validating my poetic ways
    before I did
To all at Charles C Thomas for their personal approach, a pleasure
    working with them
To Little, Brown and Company for their permission to include Ogden
    Nash's "Everybody Tells Me Everything" and "Celery"

Wordscapes

Putting life into verse,
Other pursuits could be worse!

Expressions of feeling,
Whatever's on my mind

My whole body keeling,
Meanings and messages not to stay blind

Thoughts and sentiments rise,
With words honestly given

Always that element of surprise,
My writing feels driven.

FOREWORD

Here is a package
a program of passwords
It is to bring strangers together.
　　　　　　　　—William Stafford (1991)

In *Poetic Wisdom*, artist, art therapist, budding poetry therapist, and wordsmith, Susan R. Makin, gives us a triple delight: a thoughtful treatise on the history and currency of the uses of poetry in growth and healing, an internal chap book of her poems ranging from playful to soulful and addressing her life issues in words that both echo and evoke ours, and a creative primer with which to practice accessing our own poetic wisdom.

Throughout the work, Susan's enthusiasm is the unifying thread that weaves together the disparate strands of scholarly discourse, creative disclosure and gentle teaching guide. Susan calls her poetry "word-scapes," and extols the power of writing for its capacity to provide escape from all that the modern mind goes through. How apt that word for poetry, since "scape" is akin etymologically to ship, shoulder, and shape.

Susan's poetry ships—it carries thoughts, feelings and experiences across seas of memory and pain to meaning; it helps her shoulder the burdens of life as a single woman, fully responsible for herself in today's world, and it gives shape to her sometimes formless, sometimes enormous responses to that life's demands. She has fun with the words, often using rhyme for both ordering and distancing from her emotional universe. Like Bringhurst, whom she quotes, Susan's poetic medicine "terraces, plants, and harvests time."

In her 13 years of writing, Susan has found that her poetry diminishes shame and guilt and intensifies pleasure. Drawing on the wis-

dom of a diverse array of poets and theorists in the arts and psy-
chotherapies, she entreats us to try our hand, and she shows us how.
Let this engaging book show you the beauty and value of your own
poetic wisdom as you ship, shoulder and shape your experiences,
inspired by Susan's wordscapes.

PEGGY OSNA HELLER

CONTENTS

POETIC WISDOM

INTRODUCTION

Poetry is magical—it is outside of our everyday consciousness of life; it excites an utterly unique awareness and experience.

John Briggs and Richard Monaco (1990)

Poetic Wisdom

Poetry is a word that terrifies many, because of the scholastic nightmares or sissyish connotations that it can conjure up for them. However, the art that it represents is actually entering a new era of popularity. Poetry is wise. According to Rose Solari (1996), "From hushed bookstores to competitive 'slams,' from the therapy room to the boardroom, Americans are rediscovering the power of poetry to express the truth of their lives." Solari describes how, through poem-making, human beings grow closer not only to the quiet centre of the self but also to the world around them, and discusses a resurgence of interest in poetry that has pulled poets out of their ivory towers and into the mainstream.

Germaine Greer (1995) actually quantifies poetry's growth:

> Poetry is now a special interest area, not as big as food, not as small as ice-dancing, maybe about the size of ballroom dancing. The practitioners of poetry probably outnumber the readers of poetry; in the United States the number of people registered for tax purposes as poets is more than a hundred times the number of the average print run of a book of poems.

The interest in poetry, poetry as therapy, and poetry therapy that is rapidly growing cannot be denied. Therefore, my decision to go ahead with this book is part of the new trend to demonstrate and reinforce poetry's worth. Sharing my personal poetic journey of the last 13 years, I show how mind-boggling experiences have been turned into

3

alternating moments of mindfulness and mindlessness, opportunities to check-in and occasions to vent.

Massaging The Mind

Matters concerning the mind are of significant interest to most of us. This is because whether we have something *on our mind*, or are keeping someone *in mind*, the mind's role is immense in all our lives, whoever we are, wherever we come from, and however we feel. The dictionary gives numerous definitions of mind, describing it as the element, part, substance, or process that reasons, thinks, feels, wills, perceives and judges; and psychologists' explanations of mind refer to the organism's totality of conscious and unconscious mental processes and activities (*Webster's*, 1989). For most of us, however, there is often the assumption that the mind is a determinant of intellectual power or ability. In this book, I am not so much concerned with the mind's capacities, but its well-being, a way to massage it, when required.

Massage techniques vary, from gentle, repetitive motions to controlled pauses and the application of pressure in tender areas. Massage stimulates circulation and increases suppleness (*Webster's*, 1989). With all that the modern mind goes through, in order to soothe and heal it, recent tendencies are to turn back to artistic pursuits that have proven effective since time immemorial. Therefore, an increasing number of people are literally escaping with words, or *wordscaping*.

Wordscapes, Poetry with a Small "p"

Clusters of words, whether long or short and simple or complex, expressed and arranged in imaginative order on the page, or orally, seem to touch deeper parts of both the self and others. The *wordscapes* that are ultimately created provide vistas for the mind's solace and refreshment. *Wordscapes*, a therapeutic term that I have come to coin myself, refers to what others may, traditionally, describe as poetry. They are poetry with a small "p."

Poetic Wordscaping: A Personal Testimony

The successful poem is a window through which not only do we see and re-see, but are seen and re-seen, as both writers and readers.

Anne Michaels, 1995

It has *crossed my mind* that wordscaping with poetry, while enabling me to attempt to massage my troubled or excited mind, has helped induce alternative *mind-sets*. It has given me a *good mind* to keep enough *presence of mind*, and eventually *make up my mind*, even when I felt I might be *out of my mind*.

Wordscaping has been my healer and friend since childhood. The first poem that I ever had published was at age nine, in an inter-school newspaper called Read (1968). This was quite an honour for me at the time.

Fed Up

Everybody has got something to do except me:
Mummy's gone to the hairdresser's
Daddy's on the 'phone
My friend has gone shopping
And here am I all alone.

I look back now at this poem with a strong tinge of nostalgia. Interestingly, some of the wordscapes included in Part Two of this book are merely an expansion of the loneliness theme so simply projected in this simple little verse. As a young girl, I was not aware of how much loneliness I would actually come to know in adulthood: with age, loneliness has taken me beyond feelings of being just "fed up." The written word, just as the image, is a visual record that can be looked back on at different stages of later life, and by posterity: messages, feelings and ideas, when projected by words and images, become entities that live on beyond and despite us.

Through my later childhood and early teenage years, my relationship with poetry was with reading rather than writing it, learning and reciting tomes for elocution purposes. Growing up in Liverpool, England, I had to be protected from having an accent that was too scouse (the name given to the Liverpool dialect), even though the Beatles succeeded very well despite how they sounded. In Britain in the early 1960s, B.B.C. English (proper English) was the order of the day for mobility in future years. Now, ironically, I have a Canadian accent which I find hard to shake, even in French, and am unable to conjure up *any* kind of British accent.

Since my elocution lessons were weekly and poetry reading examinations numerous, poetry was a more significant part of my daily life than I ever considered it to be at the time. However, as soon as the elocution lessons ended, so, too, did my connection with poetry. It was not until loneliness hit me again in Canada, about ten years later, that poetry's significance reemerged for me. This was when my own poems started to float to the surface. Then, subsequently, at graduate school, in an expressive therapies master's degree program, and later in interdisciplinary Ph.D. workshops, poems spontaneously deluged forth on all kinds of subjects and for all kinds of reasons. It was time to finally explore what these "creative surges" were all about, the genesis of this book.

Poetry has been my friend when no one else could be there. Poetic wisdom has been my healer when I thought I would never see the light at the end of the tunnel. It is incorrect to say that poetry has only got me through bad times; it has been very exciting when I have been able to write love poems and odes to family members and friends. A generator and receptor of both passion and joy, poetry has become an essential part of my life.

Completing a Ph.D. that focused on the use of the arts in psychotherapy not only gave me special license to indulge in poetry writing, reading and research, but also provided opportunities to meet various circles of people with whom I could share my ideas, findings, and experiences. The accomplishment of this book has not, despite my earlier and later loneliness poems, been a solitary journey, and I am appreciative to friends, acquaintances, colleagues, mentors, and family members for their overwhelming input and support.

On Reading This Book

Poetic language cannot be understood in the same way that ordinary language is understood...The words in poems are ordinary words, but something happens to them in the poem, transforms them.

John Briggs and Richard Monaco, 1990

This book can be read either from cover to cover, or dipped into. Each part, section, and chapter, though connected to the others, can equally well stand on its own. There are three main parts. The first part, "The Words Of Our Lives" explains and discusses "poetic wisdom."

The second part, "Transcripts from the Heart," contains around 200 original wordscapes divided into four sections: Relationships, Feelings, Activities, and Natural Forces. The emphasis here is on the massaging affects of poetic expression, wordscapes as therapy in action, responding to the moment. Introductory chapters provide a context for the wordscapes that follow.

The third part, "Scaping with Your Own Words" contains simple writing exercises and techniques that are intended to be stimulating and confidence-building for readers and writers of *all* levels. Lists of further resources for enthusiastic new wordscapers are also provided.

In organizing this book, I grappled with thinking about poetry in the context of western cultural expectations. According to Roland (1988), in Western culture, there is a fundamental dualism between subject and object, such as mind-body, and spirit-matter: knowledge is pursued with the goal of mastering or controlling the object but not changing the subject. However, in the East, the converse is true: knowledge is traditionally sought with the aim of transforming subjective consciousness rather than controlling the environment, man being, fundamentally, of the same substance as the rest of nature, not separate. Therefore, the subject-object relationship is much closer: nature is to be intimately lived in, as expressed through poetry and painting, rather than to be observed, judged and analyzed.

Whether westerners or easterners, this book provides points to be identified with for the curious or perplexed of both sexes as well as their therapists, teachers, friends and families. Responses to serious realities are exposed in a very nonthreatening way: through instructional commentaries, the spontaneously written wordscapes, and first-hand writing opportunities.

Thomas Moore (1994), in the introduction to his book, *Care of the Soul,* said that he was interested in taking a "humble approach," "one that is more accepting of human foibles, and indeed sees dignity and peace as emerging more from that acceptance than from any method of transcending the human condition." This book, particularly Part Two, which contains the poetry collection, intends a similar style.

It is also important to note here, that this book is written from the perspective of one who has used and uses wordscapes as therapy, not from that of a poetry therapist. In the United States, in theory, the only people who are really authorized to call themselves poetry therapists are those who have completed specific training requirements and been awarded an official designation for so doing, as prepared and administered by members of the National Association for Poetry Therapy's credentialing committee.

Now, as I send these pages out for publication I am involved in poetry therapy training to become a registered poetry therapist.

PART ONE

THE WORDS OF OUR LIVES

Whatever their subject and style, poems only get made when time and circumstances permit. Something allows them, something elicits them. They feel good being made, they feel good being read or heard, however terrifying or gentle they might be.

John Steffler, 1995

Chapter I

GETTING FROM DAY TO DAY

Human kind's perpetual existential challenges have been discussed by several psychiatrists of international prominence. Viktor Frankl (1984), the courageous Viennese holocaust survivor, states, "To live is to suffer, to survive is to find meaning in the suffering." Irvin Yalom (1989), the American clinical teacher, however, describes "This existential dilemma—a being who searches for meaning and certainty in a universe that has neither."

For Yalom, not only does a patient's confrontation with unanswerable questions expose a therapist to the same questions, but also, the therapist must recognize that the others' experiences are ultimately completely unknowable. This in mind, Anthony Storr (1992), the ground-breaking British creativity-focused author, explains the importance of the process of self-realization: the degree to which this is completed determining individuals' levels of neurosis in adult life. Noting, however, that neurosis is a subjective state, Storr, like Yalom, affirms that "Although certain aspects of a person's behaviour may enable one to deduce an inner disturbance, only the subject himself can know the extent to which he is riven by conflict."

There are challenges in every age, but today's vicissitudes are different from those of the past. The advent and speed of technological developments has not allowed man to catch up emotionally or physically, the perpetual race for a "quick fix" for whatever and however it ails testifying to this. As Robert Bly et al. (1993) declare:

We spend so much of our modern urban time shutting out the world. We are busy "getting and spending," in Wordsworth's phrase. And we are depressed,

11

focusing narrowly on our "problems." The world becomes a disturbance. It
gets in the way of what has to be done today, or it breaks into our mood with
its noisy demands. Rain is a bother; winter nights come too early; things break
down and require attention.

So, it is to ancient cures and healing rituals that the world is now turning with more confidence, poetry being one of the most demonstrably
efficient ways.

According to Bly et al. (1993), poetry can be helpful in confronting
man's existential dilemmas. They believe that we live in a "poetically
underdeveloped nation," cultural deficiencies being seen as a result of
how people live their lives: "without the fanciful delicacy and the powerful truths that poems convey, emotions and imagination flatten out."
Bly et al. have come to feel that their use of poetry and myth in mens'
groups is "a therapy of the culture at its psychic roots," helping to remedy what may lack in spirit and vision, and a loss of heart.

Bly et al. (1993) have actually opened and closed their gatherings of
men with poems for years, and through the collaboration of everyone
involved, the variety and quantity of poems employed has grown.
Their experiences have shown them how painful questions from one
poem may be answered in another. Sometimes this has even happened due to an audience member volunteering the "answering
poem." So, in this process "listeners" were able to become "tellers,"
and the "speakers" heard lines that had been forgotten or never heard
before. The poems used by Bly et al. and their men's groups' participants, have been argued over, repeated, mixed with tears and laughter, and ended events that were hard to close.

Bly et al. (1993) describe three layers of human interaction: the first
ranges from manners and kind speech to polite greetings and working
arguments; the second ranges from anger and hatred to jealousy and
acrimony; the third focuses on universal brotherhood and sisterhood
and entails peaceful coexistence. Bly et al. believe that while it is necessary for all three layers to exist for human interactions to take place,
it is the second layer that provokes most of our difficulties: "It is the
Via Negativa, the field of Conflict, the plain of Discord, the hills of
Turmoil. And, the Second Layer always exists between the First Layer
and the Third."

Describing the flip-side of the "ascending arc," Bly et al. (1993) discuss the many ancient stories describing how the time will come natu-

rally when man finds himself falling. In more modern days, holding the hand of the "Lord of Divorce," it may be "a time of crying at airports."

Thomas Moore (1993) makes a succinct list of the emotional complaints of our time that therapists hear every day in their practices. These include: emptiness, meaninglessness, vague depression, disillusionment about marriage, family and relationships, a loss of values, yearnings for personal fulfilment, and a hunger for spirituality.

Similarly, Ian Craib (1994) considers where contemporary disappointments may stem from: "In the modern world, the self is not something that is consistently rooted in the surrounding community; we each have to find our self, and given the speed of social change we have to do so regularly. The modern self is engaged in a constant exercise of self-construction and reconstruction." Craib describes how late modernity takes us beyond the bounds of mere self-control to a conception of the omnipotent, self-constructing self. This self, however, is a very weak one, because it aims at an illusion of power and satisfaction in order to protect its fragmented state.

Bly et al. (1993) believe, in fact, that the United States may have achieved "the first consistent culture of denial in the modern world." For them, denial has pervaded all levels of society. They argue that the health of any nation's soul is dependent on its adults' capabilities to face the harsh facts of the time: covering up painful internal emotions and blocking out fearful external images having become the national and private style.

> We have established, with awesome verve, the animal of denial as the guiding beast of the nation's life. The inner city collapses, and we build bad housing projects rather than face the bad education, lack of jobs, and persistent anger at black people. When the homeless increase, we build dangerous shelters rather than face the continuing decline in actual wages.

Chapter II
REBIRTHING POETRY

When I first started to wordscape, that is to read and write poetry by choice, I often thought that I was seen to be somewhat eccentric and old-fashioned by my peers. What I did not realise at the time was why I still carried on: how much relief I derived from my intimate companionship with the reading and/or making of specific poetic compositions. Today, I am comfortable and relieved that I can acknowledge my self-sustaining pastime more openly; not just because it may be fashionable, but because I am aware of its powers as a tool for comfort and growth, both personally and professionally.

According to Rose Solari (1996), public interest in poetry is at an all time high, with more choices of books, periodicals, writers' conferences, workshops, and readings than ever before. Also, the reasons for writing poetry have evolved, with writing about personal experiences being very fashionable. Solari notes that 30 years ago, critics vehemently attacked Anne Sexton for daring to mention menstruation and adulterous affairs in her poetry, whereas today's poets write for audiences eager to know their insights on experiences with racism, incest, and domestic violence. Also, there are new avenues that poets are making their way into, such as corporate training sessions, educational programs for high risk groups, therapy sessions conducted by diverse members of the psychotherapeutic community, and "poetry slams" (competitive poetry performances) held in nightclubs, bars, and theatres.

Solari (1996) comments that although there are many opinions about the new attention to poetry, there is one aspect of poetry that seems to be agreed about by everyone, "Good poetry, in whatever form, can provide a means for exploring the psychological complexities of our lives, as well as our spiritual yearnings." Nevertheless, she notes that in psychology and spirituality circles, which often turn to poetry for enlightenment and guidance, the same masters always seem to be the ones who are quoted: Rumi, Rainer Maria Rilke, T.S. Eliot, and Mary Oliver.

Solari (1996) interviewed Cornelius Eady who describes poetry as being like the blues, "'It tells the story that you know has happened to you. Spiritually, the psyche needs that.'" Eady, as the author of four books of poems, is particularly enthusiastic about the "'new attention to poetry'" in the United States because of the effect that it might have on groups whose stories have gone untold, historically: the poor, African Americans, and women.

Dan Fields (1995) notes that Bill Moyers, in his promotion of poetry on public television, calls poetry readings "'the biggest renaissance in America,'" poetry performances at that time being found in 150 places in the New York area alone. Moyers likens poetry readings to the public gatherings of early America in which citizens assembled on commons to read broad sheets and discuss the day's news. Rose Solari (1996), also refers to Moyers' public television broadcasts, states that no fewer than four programs about poetry have been produced, the most recent of which being Moyers' *The Language of Life*. In its accompanying book, Solari comments, Moyers was struck by "'how much we owe our poets for reminding us that experience is the most credible authority of all.'"

Experience, whether individual or collective, is what generates public opinion, and influences the laws, ethics, and actions of a population. Popular leanings may be political, religious, or new age, all of which have taken heed of poetical influences at some stage in their histories, no matter how significantly. The power of words themselves, no regardless of the form they might take, or the message that they project in their composition or presentation is unsurpassed, except by physical violence. Tending to be situational, words should be considered in specific context so that their magnitude can be appropriately appreciated and understood.

Rollo May (1975) declares that it is the artists (dramatists, musicians, painters, dancers, poets, and saints) who are responsible for the direct and immediate presentation of the new forms and symbols (which are poetic, aural, plastic, or dramatic). Though May emphasizes that artists live out their imaginations, expressing symbols in graphic form only dreamt about by most other human beings, he is also careful to point out how, in our appreciation of a created work, for instance, a Mozart quintet, we, too, are performing a creative act. "When we engage a painting, which we have to do especially with modern art if we are authentically to see it, we are experiencing some new moment of sensibility. Some new vision is triggered in us by our contact with the painting; something unique is born in us."

May (1975) also proposes that "just as the poet is a menace to conformity, he is also a constant threat to political dictators," and cites, as a chief example, the prosecution and purge of artists and writers under Stalin, "who was pathologically anxious when faced with the threat that the creative unconscious posed to his political system." In a similar vein, John Steffler (1995) comments on how poetry has always been a means to express human ambitions and aspirations, not only those that include dreams of "wisdom and harmony," but also those of "immortality and dominion." This being the case, he states that myths and epic fictions that point the way to action may be more than just "placebos": "Poems of war and conquest may influence a culture's endeavours. So here again the subject kaleidoscopes."

According to Arthur Lerner (1994) a founding father of poetry therapy, the poet is more able than the historian to capture the "hidden essence" of the civilization in which he lives. While the historian captures the "upper thought" of his time, as recorded in documents and state papers, the poet moves through a "hidden world" which is buried beneath the conventional wisdom of his time. Lerner (1994) notes how the early poets and art-makers, the prophets from the world's religious teachings, have connected with unexplored wisdom hidden in the unconscious for millennia.

> Their insights burst like flashes of light in some darkness. They spoke in verse, in proverbs, in parables. They did not build complete systems of thought brick on brick. They did not so much speak as they were spoken. It was as Goddeck has said of dreams. Their dark wisdom broke out in myths and parables. They rose unwilled from some depths in their lives.

Lerner (1994) is also careful to point out how the unconscious seeks meanings as opposed to knowledge, explaining that its expressions have become our "art forms." Then, in considering the early history of premodern myth-makers (mystics and poets whose spirit and messages touched later civilizations), he notes that the separation of the poet from "the world of knowledge seekers" is a comparatively recent phenomenon:

> In pre-Christian times, in the ancient worlds of Greece, Rome, and Judea, and in Persia, India, and China, men rose out of limiting civilizations in which they lived and spoke of awesome visions. Their visions seemed startlingly new for their times. And though each of these mystics lived a lifetime in isolated cultural communities, barely travelling beyond the borders of their familiar worlds, they burst forth with insights and world views never before heard in their time and place.

Similarly, May (1975) states: "Out of the encounter is born the work of art. This is true not only of painting, but of poetry and other forms of creativity," and describes how active language is in the creation of a poem.

> It is not that language is merely a tool of communication, or that we only use language to express our ideas; it is just as true that language uses us. Language is the symbolic repository of the meaningful experience of ourselves and our fellow human beings down through history, and, as such, it reaches out to grasp us in the creating of a poem.

According to Anne Michaels (1995), the distinction between knowledge and "poetic knowing" is similar to that between history and memory: "Knowledge/History is essentially amoral: events occurred. 'Poetic Knowing'/Memory is inextricably linked with morality: history's source is event, but memory's source is meaning. Often what we consciously remember is what our conscience remembers." Michaels explains how memory, like love, becomes stronger by means of restatement and reaffirmation, tradition, stories and art being good vehicles for this.

Michaels (1995) also describes how memory, whether collective or deeply personal, can haunt us until we are able to uncover the meaning that it might engender for us. She states: "When a poem successfully merges the collective and the personal, its power intensifies. Memory is elusive. We forget, we block things out. But often if not the truth then the effect of the truth emerges." Then, describing language as a "repository of cultural and personal memory," Michaels (1995) gives an example of its "emotive power": the exile who hears her mother tongue after many years, and consequently, is able to remember her childhood through rhymes and stories.

With reference to the United States, Barbara Goodrich-Dunn (1994) describes how poetry and politics are often viewed as separate entities. She discusses how, especially in the last century, poetry has become increasingly individualized, as demonstrated by "single narrators," who use it to chart their own psychological processes. She states, "Reading such work, one might imagine that politics and verse don't mix, that the business of poetry is to delineate the interior world rather than to interact with the exterior one."

In her interview with the poet Carolyn Forché, one of the key points of discussion focused on how poets in the United States might be seen to be treated differently from those in Europe. Forché offered the following observation and commentary:

> I'm not sure that it's so much that we're valued if we're seen and heard by the public, but here in the U.S. fame or notoriety is often associated with economic success. Our monetary culture has commodified almost everything. Poetry has resisted this commodification. What I see in my own culture is a tendency to value only that which is monetarily lucrative. In Europe, it seems that one is still valued as an artist apart from the degree of one's monetary success or recognition, but the globalization of monetary culture might change this.

Chapter III
POETRY

Poetry can be discussed from various perspectives. I shall consider these three. Firstly, definitions of the term itself and how the final product or art form might be viewed. Secondly, what happens in the poetry writing process and how that might be explained. Thirdly, the value imbued in spoken poetry as opposed to silent reading.

Products

There are many definitions of and opinions about what poetry is, from brief dictionary extracts to longer subjective accounts. According to *Webster's* (1989), "Poetry is lofty thought or impassioned feeling expressed in imaginative words." Beyond this definition, I see poetry as being a simple and spontaneous verbal mechanism that brings linguistic representations of both unconscious and conscious thoughts and feelings to expression (or voice) in whatever order they may arise. Surprises, confirmation and comfort may also be provided along the way through the ordering of the words and succinctness of the lines. When recorded in writing, sensations and projections surrounding what is emitted (the poetry) have the opportunity to live on, providing direct as well as symbolic meaning to the self and others.

Babette Deutsch (1974) defines the term "poetry" as, "The art which uses words as both speech and song, and, more rarely, as typographical patterns, to reveal the realities that the senses record, the feelings salute, the mind perceives, and the shaping imagination orders." Similarly, Raffel Burton's (1984) "working definition of poetry" describes, "A disciplined, compact verbal utterance, in some more or less musical mode, dealing with aspects of internal or external reality in some meaningful way." Burton (1984) also states, however, that "like all the arts, poetry is a complex meshing of substance and manner, of thought and form, of argument and technique," and notes how an artist's craft can be and usually is a deeply important part of how we react to his art.

Robert Pinsky (1988) defines poetry in its "broadest sense," and includes such forms as the short story. He also discusses the most profound and pleasurable way in which a poem engages our interest as being in the revelation of the "inward motion of another mind and soul." Then, attributing similar powers to letter-writing, he explains that he finds it impossible to write a good personal letter without going somewhat further into himself than he might do in conversation; planning and composition seeming to strip away obstacles rather than creating them.

For Anne Michaels (1995), who considers poetry's content, "The poem attempts to represent as many layers of experience as possible–unified without loss of complexity–and with luck, manages to capture an instant partially, suggestive of the whole." Also considering poetry's content, John Steffler (1995) lists some of its inclusions: "Flowers of anger, hunger, pain, hatred, and shame, even flowers of sterility and death." Steffler (1995) also gives a beautiful description of a poem and how and when it might be used: "A poem, ideally, can be carried around in the memory like a small stone in the pocket. It can be fingered for pleasure or strength or wisdom, recited, sung, turned over and over." He deems the poet to be the most skillful of all writers in the use of language, sometimes choosing obtuse and crude ways that one would employ with "concrete matter" rather than with "a system of abstract signs."

> Poetic language is fundamentally mute, a physical material very much like any physical material used for art: clay, stone, bone, wood, paint. With language the poet makes a *thing* that seems expressive of what he or she had in mind. The poem is an entity, an individual creature of words, like a sculpture, an amulet, a song. What it knows and says and *how* it knows anything are implicit and inherent in it as they are in any individual entity, a tree, a clock, an otter.

Robert Bringhurst (1995) looks at Chinese reflections on the nature of poetry, and refers to the *Shu Jing* (the *Book of History* or *Book of*

Documents) which records what the Emperor Shun is reported to have gathered from it: "'Poetry speaks *zhi*.' And *zhi* means intention, purpose, will, aspiration...one's conception of the ideal." For Bringhurst (1995), while poetry is "knowing," verse is, "a form, a technique, a device. At its most comfortable and familiar, it is structural form, like a paddler's stroke or a jogger's gait. It is the steady but adaptable lope of the mind and voice."

Exploring the nature of verse in more detail, Bringhurst (1995) discusses how, when considered "in the sense of repetitive syllabic pattern," it is rare to find it among paleolithic cultures, even though poetry may be abundant there. He states:

> Peoples who choose not to domesticate plants and animals typically choose not to domesticate language either. The hunters and gatherers I have known use language with great attentiveness and care, and they craft it with skill and dexterity–but in their oral literature, they typically accept its evolving structures and textures as a part of the terrain, like the ways of animals, the growth habit of plants, and the grain of stone and wood.

In contrast, in neolithic cultures, Bringhurst (1995) points out that plants and animals tend to be raised rather than hunted, with implements usually being made from polished stone. Also, even though more wild creatures are feared, fewer are seen with fewer still being eaten. He states:

> Peoples who plant crops in orderly rows and put animals into pens, generally speaking, make a garden of language too. Their poets and story tellers domesticate the rhythms and patterns of speech into the forms we know as verse. When cultures begin to *take dominion* over the animal, vegetable and mineral realms, they ordinarily seek dominion over the fourth kingdom, the realm of language, as well.

These comparisons in mind, Bringhurst (1995) views versification like history: "a method of terracing, planting and harvesting *time*." He remarks how more ornate and elaborate poems of verse are seldom evident in societies that do not have other elaborate technologies, in particular those which involve the smelting and casting of metal, and makes the following commentary:

> The poet and the smith have much in common in the bronze-age world, where the military aristocracy offers employment and honor to both. But elaborate

and ingenious forms of *verse*–oral high technology–are no guarantee of range or depth in *poetry*. Skill in handling these forms, like skill with software and keyboard, is no guarantee that great literature will emerge.

Molly Harrower (1995) considers one of the prerequisites of "true poetry" as transcending the immediate circumstances of its creation to have universal significance. She explains the "dual task" of the mature poet, who as well as following the natural instinct to restore personal inner balance, must also depersonalize highly charged experiences for others to be able to endow their own particular meanings on them.

Harrower (1995) also endeavours to consider when a poem might have "literary merit." She asks how one can differentiate between the "'poetic'" expression of ideas and feelings, which is essentially a communication between two parts of the self, and what is viewed as "literary": "When can a poem be considered as a creation in its own right, one with value apart from the message it gives to the writer or the relief it affords in a tension-filled situation?"

She suggests imagining "a kind of personal-universal continuum of experience," on which poems that have greater literary value might be placed at a particular point. Then, giving the example of an experience that may start as "an almost unbearable personal and idiosyncratic segment of living," she considers how it might transform over time, and find its place in "a much more universal frame of reference." Ultimately, if it loses its personal roots all together, it will almost become an "abstraction."

Considering the best poems, from a literary point of view, Harrower (1995) favours the ones which keep a degree of highly charged personal feeling, but are, nevertheless, still embedded in a more universal approach to life. Then, looking at the two polar extremes of the continuum in more detail, she comments on each of them. A poem written too close to the personal end, while being helpful in handling an overpowering experience, will be guaranteed to have too many specific references and immediate details which are insufficiently universal to become a "good' poem." A poem from which personal experiences are removed completely, however, often feels too impersonal, defensive and/or flat. For a poem to carry its lyrical message, it must arouse a genuine spark of feeling in the reader and/or listener as well as the poet.

Harrower (1995) also suggests that what the "personal-universal continuum" represents might equally be termed "an intensity gradient of emotional experience." With time and distance, the intensity of the "emotional earthquake" decreases, as does the incumbent need to communicate the raw experience of it that is sparked in the poem. Harrower (1995) describes how it is possible to measure in hours, weeks, or months, when poems have actually been written, in relation to the triggering and emotionally charged experience.

The poignancy and intensity of a situation may be so overwhelming at the moment of "emotional impact" that clarity of expression and perspective are not possible. Literary merit, then, accordingly, relates to "hypothetical optimums" of "emotional intensity" and "control" in some way.

Processes

John Steffler (1995) compares "poetry's basic method" to the practices of science, and finds that the two are not very different from each other fundamentally, in that they both require observation, analysis, and some type of expression or reporting. Where they do differ, nevertheless, is in how the observations and analyses may be carried out. Those involved in poetry can be so charged with emotion that they have a strong tendency to be ends in themselves, this being significant with respect to the emotions they awaken, not in terms of any final product.

Then, when describing how most investigations in science, despite claiming "purity," are inspired by ideas about how to alter the environment to suit human wishes, Steffler suggests that poetry's method is contrary. He sees how it is possible for it to relate to a more primitive way of coping with human longing; one that instills an appreciation in people for the way things are naturally, through the adaptation of human understanding to what is, and changes people instead of the world.

Similarly, Rose Solari (1996) stated, "In the making of poems, human beings grow closer not only to the quiet center of the self but also to the world around them." Morris R. Morrison (1987) also considers these notions further, when he describes poetry as being "adept at hypnosis and illusion; its components being frequently made up of dream, play and fictional gratification."

For Kim Maltman (1995), the moving of paint with a brush on the canvas is an inevitable part of the process of producing a picture;

though the final piece that is created is not visible in the medium while it is being made, even in the imagination. In poetry, she feels that a similar process happens. The activation of the positronic brain's language circuits is essential for the production of a poem, though what will come out is not obvious in the language used until the piece is completed. Germaine Greer (1995) states more simply, "Poetry is, of course, a matter of intellect; though the matter may be provided by the unconscious, the form must be forged and apprehended by the conscious."

Taking a practical approach, Sondra Perl (1994) asks what the connections are between the texts that we read and the lives that we live, "between composing our stories and composing ourselves." Jennifer Bosveld (1995) comments, "We are interested in a product because the product is the poet as well as the poem. Poet, poetry, poem: Patient, process, product." Similarly, Graham Greene, the novelist, sees the writing process itself to be a form of therapy, and states, "'Sometimes I wonder how all those who do not write, compose or paint can manage to escape the madness, the melancholia, the panic fear which is inherent in the human situation'" (Jamison, 1994).

Speaking Out Loud

Considering the non-written aspects of poetry, Howard Gardner (1993) states, "My belief in the centrality of the auditory—and/oral—elements in language has motivated my focus upon the poet as the user of language *par excellence*..." Similarly, Robert Bly et al. (1993) emphasize the importance of "spoken poetry": "When one reads poetry that is "all on the page," one is alone. When poetry is spoken, particularly when the larynx is opened and voice can come from the midriff, people feel in company, in joy, in community. Depths of grief are reached, and flights of inspiration."

With this in mind, Bly et al. (1993) give some advice about which poets to select for reading aloud and why. In particular, Blake is "great in a company of men," Yeats' rhetoric "penetrates to the bone," and James Wright and Anna Akhmatova "move the heart in such simple words when said quietly aloud." They also recommend David Ignatow's poems of "ordinary office and working life," and the works of D.H. Lawrence, William Carlos Williams, Etheridge Knight, Sharon Olds, Theodore Roethke, Marianne Moore, and César Vallejo.

Chapter IV
POETS

Poetry cannot be considered in isolation from those who write it. Just as some say "We are what we eat," I believe, as attested to in this book, we are what we read and write. So, who are our poets, and how do they come to poetry? What is the poetry writing experience like for them, and might there have been or are there any social constraints, such as gender, limiting their subject matter and/or prominence?

Poetic Natures

Poets can be very broadly defined today, from rock artists to advertising copy writers. I believe that everyone is touched by poetry in some way: office workers who sing along with popular songs and advertisements on the radio do not realize that they may be giving out and/or taking poetic messages in. The type of poetry ingestion facilitated by background music often promotes tacit understandings and confirmations.

Robert Bly et al. (1993), in their book, *The Rag and Bone Shop of the Heart. Poems for Men*, include William Stafford's piece, "On the Writing of Poetry." In this, Stafford states:

> A writer is not so much someone who has something to say as he is someone who has found a process that will bring about new things he would not have thought of if he had started to say them. That is, he does not draw on a reservoir; instead, he engages in an activity that brings to him a whole succession of unforeseen stories, poems, essays, plays, laws, philosophies, religions.

Bly et al. (1993) note that for Stafford to get started, he would accept anything that occurred to him, and something always did because "we cannot keep from thinking." Then, when he put something down, that thing would lead to the next, and he would be underway. He states: "If I let the process go on, things will occur to me that were not at all in my mind when I started. These things, odd or trivial as they may be, are somehow connected. And if I let them string out, surprising things will happen."

Arthur Lerner (1994) discusses the poet's gift of perception, noticing how only the poet has a very special way of knowing that it is the artist's principal gift. Looking at perception's shaping and reshaping of all manner of experience, Lerner considers perceptions being carried back and forward on a time track, a child's perceptions being captured and restated by the adult self. Therefore, we are often struck, reading the poet's renderings of his perceptions, by the recognition of long forgotten moments in our lives.

For Lerner (1994), perceptions are "private judgments of experience." There may be universal agreement on viewing the natural world, but the closer we scrutinize objects in this natural world, altering our viewing mechanisms, the more our views change. Lerner notes that the dictionary defines illusion as, "'A perception which fails to give the true character of an object perceived.'" This definition of illusion, he remarks, could also define "'delusion,'" which implies a derangement of view, suggesting that the observer is suffering some mental strain.

For Lerner (1994), both the psychoanalyst and poet, in their own ways, understand the central role played by illusion in our lives.

> When we love and when we hate, when we grow angry and when we feel compassionate depends entirely on our particular view of the experience before us...Experiences in and of themselves are neither comic nor tragic neither wrath provoking nor sorrowful. An event becomes an experience when we choose to give it our highly personal meaning. To be sure, we are expected to be sad at funerals and happy at weddings...But when we speak of ultimate meaning, it is doubtful that we share in drawing the same ultimate meaning from such experiences.

Lerner (1994) also remarks on how poets have known for centuries that a man is as he sees, and illusion, "the stuff of our lives." So, it is his conclusion that, "Those who not only know this, but who are eternally restless in searching for ever richer meanings beneath our illusions, are the poets of the world."

Morris R. Morrison (1987), one of the pioneers of poetry therapy, commented on Auden's remarks that "'writing helps us a little better to enjoy life or a little better to endure it,'" and describes this as being the mutual function of the poet and the psychotherapist. Kay Redfield Jamison (1994) looks more deeply at the significant relief that writers and artists derive from their work, "For many artists, writing or painting or composing has provided an escape from their turmoils and melancholy."

Germaine Greer (1995), on the other hand, taking a less psychological approach, indicates that the poet's bent may not be as common as others cited in this book might imply. She states, "Anyone may versify, and the results may be interesting and entertaining, but only the poet can utter poetry" (p. xiv).

Poetic Experiences

Considering poets' poetry writing experiences in general, Richard Lippin (1982) interviewed Arthur Lerner, as the pioneering poetry therapist and poet. Lerner explained how poetry intrigued him because of it being so exacting, and involved. "The condensation of feelings into appropriate poetic lines is one of the masterpieces of human invention; to be able, at a certain point, to get the exactness of a feeling, as Shakespeare did, is one of man's greatest achievements, that and language" (p. 168).

Carol Barrett (1996), a core faculty member at the Union Institute and prolific poet, in an article in *The Network* (A Publication of the Union Institute, Cincinnati, OH.), talks passionately about the writing and sharing of her poems. The related discoveries of the possibilities so given, help her to make new connections with other people. She states: "Poems became gifts—sometimes from one stranger to another. I devoured books of poems like a hungry passenger on a long train ride." Then explaining how finding the poem as a way to discover rather than remember altered the course of her writing she uses wonderful imagery: "Instead of trying to save experience, I began to pry at its edges, to see if the envelope would open. Sometimes the glue slipped easily in my hand with a single pencil. Sometimes, it seemed to be cement. I would work on a poem for years, knowing it was not yet finished; it had not yet revealed its truth."

As Barrett (1996) became more comfortable with the depth of her poems, she realised how poems could transmit emotional truths that were otherwise eluded. Then, she noticed, "The poem became an act of faith, a creation changing what is not seen into what IS seen." Finally, in answering her own question, "Why write?" Barrett states some of her many reasons, "The poet writes to romp with words, to hug and cherish, to lament and weep, to praise and celebrate, to roar with refusal, to quiet the soul."

Another Union Institute core faculty member, Clark Moustakas (1990), discusses the research of one of his supervisees, Lynne Vaughn (1989). Her study was on the experience of writing poetry, and emanated from her own discovery that some of her most painful and most joyous experiences proved inexpressible in any other form. Her most immediate resource for creative self-expression, in fact, was the lyric poem, "The Song of the Soul." After her own "immersion and attunement to writing poetry," she set out to obtain firsthand depictions of the experiences of 13 research participant poetry writers, and from her data, amongst other things, made a creative synthesis of the meanings and essence of their experiences as they had described them.

Several of Vaughn's (in Moustakas, 1990) commentaries that struck a cord with me are noted here. She recorded how: "'The poets who were interviewed for this study used metaphors to convey some of what cannot be said directly, but must be danced around to gain an understanding of what it means to write poetry...'" And, the poem was seen as "'A moment of birth—waves of letting go, of pushing out...'" Vaughn also acknowledged that, "'We poets dance around the ineffable, holding hands with the intangible. As in the experience of actually dancing, the poet moves beyond a purely physical sphere and enters into sounds within, into a communion of passion, rhythm and melody.'" Poetry writing was described, "'An encounter with mystery...An experience of living in the present moment, turning over rocks, diving into emptiness, facing insecurities, knowing special moments of connection with a loved one or with a nightfall cloaked in brilliant blue earth-shadow and wearing a halo of roses.'"

Discussing the ultimate confessional poet, Anne Sexton, David Lester and Rina Terry (1992) explain how she used her experience of married life and psychiatric hospitalizations to nurture her controversial style of writing. They comment that her 10 books attracted negative reviews because, "Some thought that she dwelt too much on the unpleasant aspects of bodily experience, such as masturbation and menstruation." Whilst there were those who considered her poems to be too confessional, others thought that they were published before having "adequate polishing."

In describing Sexton as a "preeminently confessional poet," the critics, according to Lester and Terry (1992), talked about how she wrote "in order to recover a clearer sense of who she was." The labelling of Sexton as a "minor poet, often diffuse, formless, strident, and incoherent" can, in Lester and Terry's (1992) view, be contested: "The 'confessional' mode had already been adopted by many famous poets of her era. The use of 'le moi' was being cultivated in fashionable literary journals everywhere." Sexton, Lester and Terry (1992) comment, "preferred to think of herself as an imagist based in reality rather than as a confessional poet," insisting in various interviews, "that poetry is as much fabrication as it is confession." For Sexton, "even the most brutal truth was shaped by imagination's energy and the craftman's hand."

Germaine Greer (1995), alternatively, is primarily concerned with women poets: whether they are recognized, the content and form of their writing, what role they may fill in wider society, and how the world may view them. Talking about "successful poetesses" she discusses how they retain their "affinity with childhood," not writing anything that a child would not be able to read "safely." She notes facetiously that few people would see masterpieces like Mary Had a Little Lamb, by the American poet Sara Josepha Hale, as such. According to Greer (1995), from one point of view, this is because writing and publishing for children simply took over from the "ancient female pursuit" of making up and singing poems to them, and, in accepting this, other important facts may be overlooked:

> Children's literature was part of the construction of childhood as a period of innocence and powerlessness; toys are decoys from engagement with real life and the poetry of childhood was equally phony. The literature of the nursery insisted on the nursery's separateness from the sphere of adults; no anxiety, no threat, no guilt was allowed to intrude.

In the same vein, Greer remarks on how poetesses are even more conspicuous as writers of hymns, and especially hymns for children.

Chapter V
POETIC CREATIONS

The powers of creativity, hence poetry, cannot be denied or minimized. This is confirmed by the reflections of a variety of authors who give considerable authority to the subject, irrespective of their backgrounds and/or aspects that they focus on. Creativity, whether considered in the context of madness or the unconscious, is a classic subject for discussion.

So many of us with creative bents have been considered, at least, eccentric, when staying up half the night to finish a creative project that lets us forget the passage of time and significance of anything else happening around us: we are in our own worlds. So many of us who have had occasion to wax poetic over a great sorrow in our life, using words and descriptions that seem to have popped up from nowhere, suddenly find that these words appear to make a lot of sense where and when they arise. A conscious search in the dictionary for "the right description" could never have proved as true.

Unconsciously Creative

Rollo May (1975) describes the term, "the unconscious" as "shorthand." For him, there is no such thing as "*the* unconscious,'" but rather "unconscious dimensions (or aspects or sources) of experience." He defines this unconscious as, "*the potentialities for awareness or action which the individual cannot or will not actualize,*" adding that "these potentialities are the source of what can be called 'free creativity.'"

The exploration of unconscious phenomena in relationship to creativity being a fascination for May (1975), he pondered the question,

"What are the nature and characteristics of the creativity that has its source in these unconscious depths of personality?" In considering "unconscious depths" further, May describes "unconsciousness as the depth dimension of consciousness," and "when it surges up into consciousness in this kind of polar struggle the result is an intensification of consciousness." Not only thinking capacities are heightened, but sensory processes; memory, in particular, is strengthened.

Anthony Storr (1972) discusses how when things are put into words, music or painting, what has hitherto not been fully conscious is made so. He states, "By removing what is in our minds from within to 'out there,' we alter our attitude towards these contents. A phantasy which has never been spoken or written is differently apprehended by the person who harbours it from the same phantasy when it has been objectified." Storr (1972) points out that this is not only because the form that the phantasy is now in makes it communicable to another person, but also because it has become an object that is separate from the person who created it himself, which he may actually contemplate and study, with positive or negative outcome.

Kay Redfield Jamison (1994) examines the integration of unconscious forces and more logical processes in the context of creativity, and affirms that from virtually all perspectives, those of the early Greek philosophers to twentieth century specialists, there is agreement that artistic creativity requires a dipping into prerational or irrational sources while maintaining ongoing contact with reality and "life at the surface."

> Many highly creative and accomplished writers, composers, and artists function essentially within the rational world, without losing access to their psychic "underground." Others,...are likewise privy to their unconscious streams of thought, but they must contend with unusually tumultuous and unpredictable emotions as well. The integration of these deeper, truly irrational sources with more logical processes can be a tortuous task, but, if successful, the resulting work often bears a unique stamp, a "touch of fire," for what it has been through.

For a deeper exploration of how the unconscious may influence poetry, it is important to consider Owen E. Henninger's (1994) discussion about how "poetry exposes unconscious forces to consciousness and/organizes them into an understandable form." His postulation here is that poetry is a therapeutic process, making "arrangement out of derangement, harmony out of disharmony, and order out of chaos."

> Poetry provides a camouflage that allows the writer (and reader) to ventilate unacceptable, emotionally laden ideas and unconscious conflicts. It allows these ideas and conflicts to circumvent the usual repressive barriers and come to the surface. At the same time, it exposes them to the observing ego so that they can be examined and/organized.

Henninger describes the clarity that comes from poetry as being akin to insight, enabling people to see more clearly into themselves and become more intimately familiar with their own unconscious ideas and feelings which, in turn, can provide a more honest way of looking at personal conflicts.

Madly Creative

Paul Rodenhauser (1994) describes art as a vehicle for suspending realism, a welcomer of controversy, and a provider of affirmation.

> The very same masterpieces born out of chaos can lift others to the experience of tranquillity. Although untold numbers of poets composers, novelists, and painters have endured mind-wrenching conditions, society at large seems to ponder the wisdom of tampering with its uniquely fixed members. Society not only tolerates but expects (and admires) eccentricity–if not absurdity–among its artists.

Rodenhauser then ponders the questions of the degree to which creativity itself might be curative, and wonders how medication might have affected Van Gogh's passionate brush-strokes or Byron's poetic expressions, and whether psychoanalysis enhances or stifles creativity.

Dan Wakefield (1995) declares that, "Books, academic theses, and psychological studies spew forth the message that to be creative, to be an artist, you must be neurotic or nutty, or become so in the process." However, after talking to a variety of creators, he found the contrary to be true; creation seems to bring people to life and awaken the spirit.

> Commentators of all kinds who promote the mythical glamour of the doomed artist, psychoanalyzing art into an expression of neurosis, seldom if ever mention the central, key factor of the creative experience: the incomparable joy of

it, not the illusory bubble of fame but what Robert Henri calls "the happiness that is in the making."

Even when Wakefield himself has written about a painful time or situation, capturing it in words seems to provide a sense of triumph over it, with it becoming more understandable through the beauty of language, as a "piece of art."

Kay Redfield Jamison (1994), an acclaimed professor of psychiatry who is also a sufferer of manic-depressive illness, engaged in several studies which explored connections between accomplished creative persons and the prevalence of mood disorders. Her study of the rates of mood disorders, suicide and institutionalization in a sample of British and Irish poets who lived between 1705 and 1805 revealed that more than one half seemed to show strong evidence of mood disorders. Jamison listed 13 (one out of three) who seemed likely to have suffered from manic depressive illness: Christopher Smart, William Cowper, George Daley, Robert Fergusson, Thomas Chatterton, William Blake, Samuel Taylor Coleridge, (George Gordon) Lord Byron, Percy Bysshe Shelley, John Clare, Hartley Coleridge, Thomas Lovell Beddoes, and James Clarence Mangan. Out of these 13, two committed suicide, and four were committed to asylums.

Jamison's (1994) study of 47 eminent contemporary British writers and artists (selected because they had won at least one prestigious award in their field), focused primarily on the role of moods in the creative process, not on psychopathology. In this context, it considered rates of treatment for mood disorders, seasonal patterns of moods and productivity, the nature of intensely creative episodes and hypomania, and the perceived role of very intense moods with respect to works produced.

Jamison (1994) found that 38 percent of the writers and artists in the study actually had been treated for mood disorders, three quarters of whom were medicated or hospitalized. Poets showed the highest rates (33 percent) for requiring medical treatment for depression. Playwrights showed the highest total rate of treatment for depression (63 percent), though more than half underwent psychotherapy on its own (not being medicated). Prolonged elated states were more frequently reported by novelists and poets, and severe mood swings by playwrights and artists.

Virtually all the creative writers and artists in the study (89 percent) reported experiencing "'intensely creative episodes" usually of two weeks' duration. These were "characterized by increases in enthusiasm, energy, self-confidence, speed of mental association, fluency of thoughts and elevated mood, and a strong sense of well-being." Nine out of ten of the subjects studied said that these very intense moods were integral and necessary (60 percent) or very important (30 percent). Also, "Consistent with their higher rate of medical treatment for mood disorders, more poets than any other group regarded these moods as essential to what they did and how they did it."

Anthony Storr (1972) describes the creative individual as one who possesses an unusual combination of qualities, and a "tension between these opposites" which provides the motivating force for creation to take place. Needing to have the capacities to access his own inner depths, he must also have an adequate degree of control over containing and making use of what is to be found there. "Creative people," he comments, "habitually describe their dependence for inspiration upon sources outside their conscious volition. Moreover, creative people show a wider than usual division in the mind, an accentuation of opposites." Storr (1972) is also careful to point out that, "It is important to make a clear distinction between illness and character structure. A man may have a manic-depressive psychopathology without being clinically ill or having any kind of breakdown."

Chapter VI
POETRY AS THERAPY

The distinction between poetry as therapy and the field of poetry therapy is an important one to explore. Poetry may be used as therapy by anyone, but not all poetry used as therapy can be described as poetry therapy. Similarly, the designation of poetry therapist should not be assumed freely by those who apply poetry therapeutically. This is irrespective of the fact that their practice might be in developmental or clinical settings. As the field of poetry therapy emerges, so too do "territorial rights." Modern society mandates recognition through specialized training, and certification opens doors. Poetry therapy, as a profession, is currently establishing its place, privileges, and priorities in the United States.

History

Poetry therapy pioneer and physician, Jack Leedy (1985) traces the early history of poetry in medical practice back to the Stone Age shaman, whom he cites as being the first to incorporate it into his healing rituals through spells, exhortation, and the rites of exorcism. Leedy (1985) also noted how poetry played a key role in the medical approaches of the ancient civilizations: the Mesopotamian, Babylonian, Greek, Roman, Hebrew, Etruscan, Arab, Teutonic, and Celtic cultures. Remarking on anthropological evidence that, "bears witness to the surviving place of poetry in medical practice in disparate areas across the globe," he listed Siberia, the Orient, Polynesia, Australia, Africa, the American-Indian and Eskimo cultures, and commented that "peasant and surviving primitive communities" are still seen to identify poetry with healing.

The National Association for Poetry Therapy's "Guide to Training Requirements for Credentialing as a Poetry Therapist" (1993) records how it is not surprising that Apollo is the god of poetry, as well as of medicine, medicine and the arts being historically entwined. In the Guide (1993), poetry used for healing and personal growth purposes is traced back as far as the fourth millennium, B.C. "In ancient Egypt, words were written on papyrus and then dissolved into a solution so that the words could be physically ingested by the patient to take effect as quickly as possible. It is also noted that "the first poetry therapist on record" was a Roman physician called Soranus, who lived in the first century A.D. He was known for prescribing tragedy for manic patients, and comedy for depressed patients.

Bibliotherapy, the Guide (1993) notes, existed in the United States as early as the 1840s, when Dr. Benjamin Rush, called the "father of American psychiatry," is attributed with having introduced reading and writing as well as music into the Pennsylvania Hospital, the first hospital in the United States (founded by Ben Franklin in 1751). In those days, they were primarily offered as self-directed recreational tasks, and patients were able to publish their work in *The Illuminator*, their own newspaper.

According to the Guide (1993), the term *bibliotherapy* is more widely known than *poetry therapy* which only became popular in the 1960s and 1970s, as will be elaborated on later in this section. "Bibliotherapy literally means books, or literature to serve, or help medically. Poetry therapy is a specific and powerful form of bibliotherapy, unique in its use of metaphor, imagery, rhythm, and other poetic devices." Also, poetry, being seen as an art form, its inclusion in the term *poetry therapy*, helps in the definition of the field as a *creative arts therapy* like the art, music, dance and drama therapies. Today, to allay any confusion, the terms *bibliotherapy* and *poetry therapy* are usually used interchangeably, as is the case with *movement therapy* and *dance therapy*.

The Guide (1993) records that Samuel Crothers is identified as the first person to have coined the term "*bibliotherapy*" in 1916. Librarians were the first to use it, seeing the value of their practice of selecting and using books helpful to psychiatric patients. Initially, *bibliotherapy* was the use of "informational books" and "selected imaginative novels" whose characters might serve as "models or warnings" for the reader. Close collaboration was fostered between the Menninger doctors (of Topeka, Kansas), and hospital librarians, who they felt knew the literature that might "draw the patients out." However, although librarians kept the term *bibliotherapy* alive, their services offered no provision for planned discussion of readers' personal reactions to materials.

In 1928, the Guide (1993) notes that Eli Greifer, who was both a pharmacist and lawyer by profession, but an inspired poet through passion, began an enthusiastic campaign to show how a poem's didactic message can have healing powers. A resident of New York, he was an organizer of the Village Arts Centre and the Messagists Club, and created the "Remedy Rhyme Gallery." He also created a "poemtherapy" group at Creedmore in the 1950s, and, in 1959, facilitated a poetry therapy group at the Cumberland Hospital with two supervising psychiatrists, Dr. Jack Leedy, and Dr. Sam Spector. After Greifer's death in 1966, his love of "poem therapy" was further developed by Leedy, who was instrumental in creating the Association for Poetry Therapy.

Pioneering poetry therapists came from backgrounds both inside and outside of medicine. Unfortunately, it is not possible to mention all contributors in such a brief account. References to a number of other notable initiators of the discipline, however, can be found throughout this book. The six individuals noted here are discussed in the Guide (1993) and have been selected in combination for their demonstration of diverse interests and approaches in the field as it emerged. They are: Joy Shieman from California, whose pioneering research in 1962 involved a method called "therapoetics"; Ruth Lisa Schechter, who became the first official poetry therapist at Odyssey House in New York City in 1971, working with addiction and victims of rape and incest; librarian Eloise Richardson, who convinced the Governor of Baltimore to hold a Poetry Therapy Day which was sponsored by the state of Maryland in 1974; poet and educator, Aaron Kramer, who specialized in working with the deaf and disturbed; poet Art Berger, who used rock and blues lyrics, and "jazz cinquaines" to elicit writing from children; and Dr. George Bell, a minister from Ohio, who incorporated poetry into his counseling, developing "the feedback poem."

Significant pioneering figures in the world of psychology who have recognized the importance of the relationship between the arts and healing include Freud, Adler, Jung, Arieti, and Reik. Moreno is credited with having introduced the terms "*psychopoetry*" and "*psychodrama.*" However, according to the Guide (1993), it was not until the 1960s (when the term poetry therapy emerged) that "interactive processes" were introduced in bibliotherapy: at this time, group therapy was becoming a popular model for treatment. In group sessions, a number of mental health professionals from a variety of disciplines started to introduce poetry therapy techniques which reflected and reinforced their own interests in the therapeutic properties of literature. In due course, universal validation for these professionals' approaches and discoveries was provided, with the subsequent necessity for devising and recognizing specialized training courses.

Today, the National Association for Poetry Therapy, which is discussed in the third part of this book, confers professional credentials on biblio/poetry therapists who have met rigorous training criteria involving the instruction of appropriate ways to guide others in their use of literature and writing techniques. According to the N.A.P.T. Advisory Committee (1995), today's poetry therapist needs to be knowledgeable about psychological theory and group dynamics as well as literature. Contemporary poetry therapy occurs in a variety of settings, and The N.A.P.T. keeps a registry of biblio/poetry therapy practitioners in educational, medical, geriatric, therapeutic and community facilities.

Incidentally, music for therapeutic purposes, as mentioned earlier in this section, was introduced at the Pennsylvania Hospital at the same time as poetry. Music therapy, however, is already a well-established and accepted profession today, both in the United States and elsewhere.

Explanations

As explained in the previous section, the terms "*Poetry therapy*" and "*bibliotherapy*" are synonymous, and according to the N.A.P.T.'s Advisory Committee (1995), they refer to the intentional use of poetry and other literary forms for assistance in healing and/or for personal growth.

Imaginative literary material—books; articles; stories; songs; poems; films or videos may be chosen to elicit both thoughts and feelings. The therapeutic experience is facilitated by a therapist, poet, or other professional trained in biblio/poetry therapy and may involve a one-to-one relationship, a couple, a family, or group process.

Catharsis, which means to cleanse through emotional release, is central to the poetry therapy process. Also important is the development of and/or involvement with a transitional object. Peggy Heller (1995), the director of the Poetry Therapy Training Institute, refers to Winnicott's "transitional space," "that space between fantasy and reality where play, change and creativity can take place." In art therapy, the art object created, which serves as a transitional object, can both significantly affect and be significantly affected by transference/countertransference relationships (Makin, 1994).

According to its Advisory Committee (1995), the N.A.P.T. defines and endorses two specific types of poetry therapy practice, *Developmental Interactive Bibliotherapy* and *Clinical Interactive Bibliotherapy*. *Developmental Interactive Bibliotherapy* is distinguished as being the domain of "healthy populations," and practiced primarily in schools, recreation centres, libraries, nursing homes and the like. Poetry therapists who have completed training requirements to work with these populations are given the designation of Certified Poetry Therapist (C.P.T.). *Clinical Interactive Bibliotherapy*, in contrast, is employed in clinical settings such as psychiatric units, community mental health centres, and chemical dependency units. Poetry therapists who have completed training requirements to work in these settings are given the designation of Registered Poetry Therapist (R.P.T.), and, apart from their specialized poetry therapy training, have a master's or doctoral degree in a mental health profession.

The description of poetry therapy that follows, as provided by the Advisory Committee (1995), applies to that practiced by both types of practitioner.

Poetry therapy is an interactive process with three essential components: the literature, the trained facilitator, and the client(s). A trained biblio/poetry therapist selects a poem or other form of written or spoken media to serve as a catalyst and evoke feeling responses for discussion. The interactive process helps the individual develop on emotional, cognitive, and social levels. The focus is on the person's reaction to the literature, never losing sight of the primary objective—the psychological health and well-being of the client.

Also, both types of poetry therapy practitioners may use techniques such as creative writing, journaling, and/or life review and reminiscence to stimulate participants' own original writing which facilitates ends such as self-discovery, self-affirmation, reflection and insight.

According to the Advisory Committee (1995), literature's power rests largely on symbolic representation through metaphor, and how and why people identify with characters, situations, and solutions contained in it. Therefore, the selections used are not chosen for their literary merit, but for the potential that they may have in arousing self-awareness, confirming issues, and suggesting possibilities for growth and/or change. Also, when participants externalize details about their feelings, events, and thoughts by describing and recording them in writing, the act of so doing not only gives them a sense of mastery, but also allows them to view things from a different perspective. "Often people who are experiencing loss or stress are comforted by a poem or affirming thought that they can carry with them."

Poetry therapy, like art therapy, may be experienced as being less confrontational or threatening than conventional therapies because of its subtlety. Given that poetry has the potential to conceal as well as reveal, due to the possibility of layers of meaning and paradoxical tendencies, participants have more opportunity to freely express themselves without being judged (Makin, 1994). Peggy Heller (1994), in her clinical practice, notes how poetry writing has enabled "survivors" to "maintain an illusion of self-soothing safety, or a rageful, screaming intensity that reveals what cannot be said, or a factual reality-based reporting to clarify what is too confusing."

The Advisory Committee (1995) explains how an agenda for a session is suggested by the introduction of a particular poem, which a group may evade if they are not ready for it. Alternatively, when participants hear a group member read or write from the heart, they may feel more encouraged to do so themselves. The honesty extolled through poetry and other creative writings, and challenges that it offers, helps people to explore otherwise avoided difficult issues. "The process of reading and writing, encouraged by the sensitive guidance of professionals trained in bibliotherapy, acts as a catalyst for self-integration."

The Advisory Committee, nevertheless, makes a point of listing certain types of literature that should be avoided, the use of which would be countertherapeutic. Material that is confusing, hopeless, and depressing or offers no resolution or insights into coping with negative feelings (even if a poem's last few lines might be uplifting), as well as material that glorifies homicide or suicide, and denigrates parental figures or God may cause countertherapeutic results. The poetry therapist must also pay special attention to ensure that the content of material presented be relevant to the group's participants, respecting their developmental levels, cultural make-up, literacy levels, circumstances, and emotional fragility. It is also recommended that the poetry therapist not include his or her own written work, published or unpublished. Peggy Heller (1994) notes, "Since I carefully choose literature that not only deals with issues relevant to the clients' treatment, but also stresses empowerment and the restoration of hope, most participants do not feel threatened and want to proceed."

The Advisory Committee (1995) suggests that under ideal conditions, each participant should be given a copy of the literature that has been chosen, so that the words may be absorbed visually and aurally at the same time. The silent reading of poetry prevents the appreciation of rhythm, rhyme, assonance, alliteration and the like, which all contribute to the appropriate projection of a poem's meaning(s). Reading poetry aloud, in a group in particular, helps build cohesion, and can be ego-boosting for both the participant reader and respondees.

A Poem A Day Keeps The Doctor Away

Molly Harrower (1995), discussing the theme of her book, *The Therapy of Poetry*, points out immediately that she sees poetry not so much as a tool for use in formal therapy, but as "therapy" itself, and "part and parcel of normal development." She describes poetry therapy as a "newcomer," noting how poets existed long before therapists. From time immemorial, in struggling to cope with his "inevitable inner turmoil," man has used ballads, songs, and poems.

> Once crystallized into words, all engulfing feelings become manageable, and once challenged into explicitness, the burden of the incommunicable becomes less heavy. The very act of creating is a self-sustaining experience, and in the poetic moment the self becomes both the ministering "therapist" and the comforted "patient." One can afford to be hurt, one can afford to reach for the stars, if there is a built-in safeguard against crippling depression or disorganizing excitement.

According to Arthur Lerner and Ursula Mahlendorf (1992), in the introduction of the book that they edited, *Life Guidance Through Literature:* "Insightful contemporary writers are keen observers of others, of their age, of their society, and of themselves. They are therefore eminently well qualified to advise us on our society's most pressing problems. If we learn to read them well, we can benefit from their insights."

In answering the question why fiction, whether in print or on film and video, should be able to guide us in difficult life situations, Lerner and Mahlendorf (1992) consider how writers of fiction construct a whole world in each work, incorporating observations of persons and events, as well as values and ideas, from their own experiences and world views. Then, explaining how research on the working of the human mind tells us that we all construct our worlds from our experience, they note how writers can enrich each of our limited individual self-constructed worlds with their wider, and even mature perspectives.

> Literature as instruction can provide positive models of behavior. It can also illustrate self-destructive or self-defeating behavior– if we can be helped to recognize the signs of such behavior. In this way, literature can change our ideas about life and make us more sensitive to those of others.

Jack Leedy (1985) also provides some valuable commentaries about the curative properties of literature. He records how Robert Graves noted that "'A well-chosen anthology of verse is a complete dispensary for the more common mental disorders and may be used as much for prevention as cure,'" He also then cites Norman Cousins' description of the human brain as "'an apothecary capable of writing prescriptions for the human body. Cousins adds, "'Many of the patient's problems are better comprehended through the realm bequeathed by art and literature than through the facts revealed by science.'"

Arthur Lerner (1994) notes that in the "pantheon of procedures known as psychotherapy," historically, one of the most important and/or common has been recourse to the written rather than the spoken word. He states, "For generations, people have gone to the Bible for solace, comfort and guidance, and have been sustained in their troubles and problems not only by the messages in the words but also by the sonority and harmony of words, as represented in common prayers." Then, considering poetry, he acknowledges how it can play "a very special part" in the psychotherapeutic process: poems tend to be short, and are often constructed in a way in which they appeal to emotions and "can aim for a central point like an arrow to a bull's-eye."

Poem-Making

Molly Harrower (1995) believes that to understand the therapy of poetry, it must be studied in particular context, as an integral part of the stage of development that an individual has reached. She feels that the first version of a poem created in adulthood is often the result of too much pressure, when it is imperative to say something at all costs and reach outwardly quickly. Here, the controls of form, economy of wording, and need for clarity do not always operate well. So, a second version may be produced that offers a better balance between the need to express and the how of this expression. Poems of adolescence, on the other hand, according to Harrower's (1995) research samples, are rarely revised, the highly charged emotional experiences with all their personal connotations being ends in themselves.

Harrower (1995) compares poems written in the therapeutic setting of "poetry therapy" as having these too personal and adolescent qualities, carefully adding that while many poems written within the framework of formal therapeutic experiences have merit as poems, many do not.

Speaking from the perspective of a psychologist who is interested both in therapy and in poetry, Harrower says that while it may be of "epoch-making importance" to a patient's development that he be able to express some buried feeling in a form other than prose, this does not make the product "*poetry*." She is of the opinion that poems, just like people, grow and mature, and wonders if there has been a lack of attention to stages of this growth, due to a need in all of us to "conceive of poems as a gift form the poetic muse."

Harrower also discusses the "soul-searching efforts of the adolescent" and adolescent poetry in more detail, which seems to confront problems and inner turmoil head on.

One knows exactly what crisis the individual is facing. The poems clearly attempt an integration of the new, and often ego-threatening, life experience,

with the old and more sanguine beliefs. The poem restores an inner balance
by both acknowledging, and going beyond, the new information that has to be
absorbed.

Harrower (1995) herself writes poems for a number of reasons:
because they solve a conflict, because she is ill at ease spiritually and
wants to clarify her thoughts and feelings, and because she is driven to
create order from some inner chaos. Her poems come when she is
flooded and overpowered by feelings which have been provoked by
some aspect of life or nature. Allowing some "intellectual craftsmanship" helps subdue the all-pervading emotions which control her and
help in the formulation of "manageable thoughts." She states, "This
great bulk of feeling can only be subdued or brought under control if
I allow some intellectual craftsmanship to work on it, to produce a
manageable thought which I can control in the place of the all-pervading emotions which control me."

Harrower (1995) is aware that conflicts take different forms at different stages of one's development. However, regardless of the stage
that one is at or nature of the conflict, she sees the very fact that it is
being expressed as a positive step in the face of obvious dilemma.
Making reference to Melville Cane, Harrower says that he expresses
similar ideas to her own, writing of the need to share a poem utilizing
or converting emotional shock from its negative content to something
positive and constructive.

Harrower (1995) contends that one of the functions of poetry is to
restore an inner balance that has temporarily been lost: "The writing
of the poem seems to provide comfort when external solace is lacking.
The poem reactivates memories or experiences which have given
meaning and value to life." Interestingly enough, she points out that
despite no apparent conscious motivations when writing, looking back
many years later at poems created during times of stress, loneliness
and sadness, how it is possible to detect "self-therapeutic trends":

As a result of the reactivation of memory and meaningful moments, the vulnerable part of the self is able to shift the psychic point of departure. Loneliness
or despair are no longer the paramount feelings, rather there is a challenge to
'recapture heights.' Thus a period of potentially stagnating depression may be
averted, and the individual reoriented to more positive goals.

Harrower (1995) is careful to acknowledge that depression is triggered not only by the loss of a loved person, nor are the only conflicts

experienced those directly connected with other persons. In her opinion, one of the most effective uses of poetry from the self-therapeutic
point of view is for the objectification of any hampering experience
afforded by it. When we are able to objectify, the externalization helps
the poet rise above the "emotional morass." However, Harrower cannot stress strongly enough, her surprise about her lack of "editorial
awareness" when actually writing. Though poems emerge from strong
feelings which need to be dealt with, any self-therapeutic purpose is
usually not obvious to the writer.

Harrower (1995) suggests that self-sustaining aspects of poetry might
also be seen as part of an individual's struggle to achieve or maintain
personal integrity:

> Poems are written during personal crises; they are not written with the *explicit*
> wish to triumph over adversity, yet, in their execution and achievement they
> reaffirm the "dignity of the lifestyle." Once achieved, they consolidate the posi-
> tion, reinforce the ground gained against despair and meaninglessness.

PART TWO
TRANSCRIPTS FROM THE HEART

Psychology has moved into matters that used to be left to poetry.
Rollo May, 1993

Chapter I

"I'VE BEEN THERE TOO"

Being able to say "I've been there too!" provides welcome companionship. Edith Wallace (1982), when introducing a poem by Peggy Pond Church, whose poetry affected her deeply, said: "I hope the following poem will evoke the response in you that it did in me and many others. To be moved, to be touched is always a healing experience; without this emotional interaction no healing can take place."

At various points, the reader may be comforted, saddened, informed, angered, amused or intrigued by the different feelings and conditions focused on by particular wordscapes in this part of the book. The courage to acknowledge awkward sentiments is seldom easy to find, and it is sometimes hard to be honest with ourselves if we know that our sense of hope might be challenged. Then, when someone else seems to express our own repressed feelings directly, in concise poetic terms, reactions may be tempered by confusion, resentment or relief.

Dinora Pines (1993), one of Britain's leading psychoanalysts, made the following statement:

> Love, joy and pleasure in living both for oneself and for other people are aspects of human experience which are easily expressed. What remain secret and unknown, in order to avoid shame and guilt, is the child's fear of abandonment, of being unlovable, the fear of loneliness, and lifelong struggle to come to terms with one's own mortality.

Over the course of 13 years (1984 - 1997), I had ample opportunity, spontaneously turning to poetry for self-help, to draw to the surface

49

what Pines described as remaining "secret and unknown." In this
process, I discovered how poetic expression not only softens admis-
sions of shame and guilt, but can also confirm and intensify loves, joys
and pleasures.

Chapter II
"DOWN IN THE DUMPS"

The wordscapes included here have the potential to be highly evocative, expressing painful, buried and disowned feelings that we are frequently too embarrassed or ashamed to acknowledge. Unfortunately, people tend to seek answers and solace in more distressing rather than happier states and times. This is when they turn to therapy. In fact, since I wrote many of the poems included here (unknowingly) for my own self help, that the percentage of less cheerful ones is higher is not surprising.

Doriane Laux (1995) writes about her own poetry writing experience in the foreword to Steve Kowit's book, *In the Palm of Your Hand, The Poet's Portable Workshop.*

Who knows which step will lead you into the rest of your life? I don't know if poetry can change the world, but I do know that as I read it and wrote it, my life began to change; I began to develop a feeling of intimacy with the world around me, an umbilical connection to other minds, other voices, other hearts. It was as if I were being given a map of the soul, an emotional history of the world.

Germaine Greer (1995) proposes that, "The more powerful, gifted or passionate the woman, the more inevitable the agony," and makes a lengthy treatise on the subject:

The female poet is not presented with the women's magazine standby of a choice between marriage and a career, but with the choice to be happy and mute or unhappy and articulate. Happy marriage and motherhood are not the raw material of poetry, let alone poetry of high seriousness.

51

Greer (1995) cites Couzyn who believed that the happy woman had nothing to say, and comments that only now does it seem that the situation is changing. In showing this, she includes some lines written wryly by Stevie Smith:

Why does my Muse only speak when she is unhappy?
She does not, I only listen when I am unhappy
When I am happy I live and despise writing
For my Muse this cannot but be dispiriting.

Greer (1995), herself, is quick to add, "This is not to say that the woman poet must manufacture unhappiness, but rather that unhappy women will be attracted to poetry and that poetry will give their unhappiness permanent form in intransigent text."
Alternatively, for Molly Harrower (1995), psychological health is ultimately bound up with how we relate to others. She states, "No restoring or sustaining process can occur if it does not relate one in some way to another person." However, how this comes about matters: for a "potentially unwieldy mass of feeling" to become intelligible to another person, it must lose any unstructured completely egocentric aspect. For example, "warding-off-depression" poems are effective in this endeavour if they "become a triumphant rather than defeatist gesture," seeming to say, "I am not alone if it is known that I can stand being alone."
On a different note, Kay Redfield Jamison (1994) points to the irony associated with artistic flowering at less cheerful times. She explains how melancholy's association with artistic inspiration and productivity is contrary to what we would expect: a slower pace usually being forced, ardour cooled, and perspective being given to thoughts, observations, and feelings from better times. With the authority of recent research, Jamison (1994) acknowledges how observations and beliefs produced during mildly depressed states may actually be closer to "'reality'" than those emitted during "normal mood states," the pervasiveness of denial in everyday life being emphasized. This concurs with Bly et al's postulations in Part One, Chapter One of this book.

Chapter III
GETTING PERSONAL

Irvin Yalom (1989) stated that, "Our life, our existence, will always be riveted to death, love to loss, freedom to fear, and growth to separation. We are, all of us, in this together." There is nothing to beat the relaying of personal experience, and that which is taken to be deeply personal, more often than not, is universally felt. In the poetry selection included here, poems stemming from conversations with others are interspersed freely with poems that have emerged from my personal experiences. My intention is not to be a sole commentator, but to express common sentiments from the particular era and generation to which I belong.

That I chose to include my own wordscapes, exclusively, in this part of the book, was a risk, making me feel very exposed. However, after reading Molly Harrower's book, *The Therapy of Poetry* (1995), I was reassured that my instinct to do so was right. At the beginning of her text, Harrower explained her personal rationale for taking a similar course. She believes that to understand poetry's "self-sustaining features" and relation to personal growth, it is important "to know the inside story," that is the general and specific conditions that trigger the idea of writing a particular poem and its execution.

Harrower (1995) acknowledges that even though some interesting psychoanalytically-oriented postmortems of the works of well-known authors have been made, the poets themselves have seldom done their own reviews. In any event, for those considering poetry from an aesthetic point of view, knowing the "inside story" may not be relevant (and my wordscapes should not be considered for any aesthetic value). Harrower points out that only a minority of poets have any intense interest in their psychological processes per se. She also acknowledges how the reader's enjoyment of the poem itself could possibly be detracted from if too much is known about the conditions surrounding the writing of it.

With Harrower's explanations in mind, it is important for me to mention here that the collection of poetry that follows, though it is not essentially autobiography, does have much autobiographical relevance. Therefore, the individual poems are not organized chronologically, and the fact that their dates and writing contexts are excluded is only intentional. Also, any names or locations that might be identifiable have been changed.

In the Toronto daily newspaper, *The Globe and Mail,* Margaret Wente (1994), in her column, "Women," discussed the poetry of "The Thinking Woman's Heartthrob," Leonard Cohen, finding that her feelings for him go back 25 years: "We discovered him at the same time we discovered all of life's other great verities—Art, love and vague but powerful spiritual yearnings. Most of the time it was hard to tell which was which, but Leonard's poetry gave legitimacy to them all." I hope that the wordscapes that you choose to read from this collection help to legitimize some of your verities too.

Chapter IV

PARADOX

Richard Lippin (1982) records that poetry intrigues Arthur Lerner because it is so exacting and involved. Lerner describes how the condensation of feelings into appropriate poetic lines is one of the "masterpieces of human invention." My biggest challenge in assembling the collection of wordscapes included here did not come from the crafting or editing of appropriate poetic lines, but from the devising of the four separate sections: "Relationships," "Feelings," "Activities," and "Natural Forces." Then, in turn, the individual wordscapes selected needed to be organized within the different chapters' subdivisions.

One of the essential things about poetry is its ability to hold paradox. John Fox, the author of *Finding What You Didn't Lose. Expressing Your Truth and Creativity Through Poem-Making* (1995), reminded me of this one day when I was grappling with revising the chapter headings and placements of the individual wordscapes within the separate sections for this book. For instance, a wordscape about effusive poetry writing may also be one about sharing disappointment, as the following example demonstrates:

This Poetry Pours From My Head

All this poetry pours from my head,
I'd rather be doing something else instead!

All this poetry causes me to stop and think,
It's hard to see some of my thoughts in ink!

Carried away in the moment,
I'd like to be
But, carried away in the moment,
Of relief, no guarantee

Enjoying the moment, I'd like to
Why can't it work for me as it does for you?

My verses are not meant to chastise,
It's only fair to share what's behind these eyes.

Chapter V

SINGLEDOM, THE NEW MID-LIFE CRISIS

Mid-life singledom is a prominent theme in the wordscapes that follow. Herbert Strean (1995), in his book, *Therapy with the Unattached,* discusses the necessity of sensitive and appropriate approaches to treatment with today's very prominent "singles" populations. He reports that mental health professionals, regardless of the setting in which they practice and therapeutic theories and modalities that they favour, all agree that their "modal patient" is the unattached person, and takes an "unequivocal position": "To love and be loved by a mate is a healthier, more fulfilling, more pleasureful modus vivendi than to live alone." Turning to supportive empirical evidence, he stresses that, "No man can be an independent island and concomitantly feel happy."

Strean's comments in mind, it is appropriate to mention here the not uncommon current abundance of single women in their late 30s whose struggles are a recurrent theme in this poetry collection (because, at the time of writing, I am one of them). Many of the mood states, dilemmas, and reactions described here may well be identified with to greater and lesser degrees by other females of the same age group, and in similar circumstances. In times of transition and under less than favourable conditions, it is important to know that we are not alone, and that life does have its happier and more humourous moments. There are many trials and tribulations as well as joys to be experienced at this stage in life, and there are ways to "muddle through!"

For most single females in their late 30s, love or the absence of it is often a major preoccupation, as attested to in the many poems concerned with it in this collection. Like Strean, Viktor Frankl (1984) offers justification for any over-attention to the focus on love, or the absence of its possibility in the wordscapes collection that follows.

> A thought transfixed me: for the first time in my life I saw the truth as it is set into song by so many poets, proclaimed as the final wisdom by so many thinkers. The truth—that love is the ultimate and the highest goal to which man can aspire. Then I grasped the meaning of the greatest secret that human poetry and human thought and belief have to impart: *The salvation of man is through love and in love.* I understand how a man who has nothing left in this world still may know bliss, be it only for a brief moment in the contemplation of his beloved.

Molly Harrower (1995) talks about how an important part of many therapeutic experiences concerned with "the guided exploration of the searching self," is the coming to terms with "dependent needs." She asks, "To what extent have love relationships been unsatisfactory for a woman because she has not been able to experience genuine submission?" In responding to this question, she notes how our world validates women's assumption of significant and superior roles in professional fields. Consequently, there is the danger that the "basic component of submitting to master" may have been lost or never realized. Love that has been lost or never realized is often expressed in the poetic musings of those who grieve for fulfilling relationships.

Chapter VI

AN INTRODUCTION TO THE WORDSCAPES
COLLECTION

In reviewing the wordscapes collection that follows, I realised two considerations. Firstly, that the reader should know a little more about what to expect concerning my style of writing as a poet, and how I and others might feel about it. Secondly, that an overview should be given of what is contained in the various parts, sections and chapters; what might be seen as being the natural progression between them, and individually significant aspects.

The Wordscaper, Herself

Acrostics in Time

Susan
1992

Behind the **S**mile
     Rest **U**nknown Qualities
And thought**S** that
     CAnnot
Be show**N**

Susan
1997

Supporting
Unconventional
Special
Artistic
Notions

As a prelude to entering the wordscapes collection, I feel that it is important to say a little more about myself; this time as wordscaper. When responding to the final draft of my Ph.D. dissertation, the second reader on my committee, Dr. Stan Searl, asked what I found to be intriguing questions, "Who are your poetic mothers and fathers? Where do you place yourself in the world of poetry?" He then went on to draw comparisons between my work and that of Ogden Nash and Edgar Allen Poe, respectively.

Until Stan had drawn these poets and their works to my attention, I had never considered my poetry to follow anyone else's styles. Yes, I was very aware that most of my verses tend to rhyme and involve couplets and repetition. However, more recently I was conscious of fighting all three devices (the rhyme, couplets, and repetition). I don't plan my poetry, it just seems to come out this way, contrary to the practices of those "good poets" whom I had read to that date. I only forgave my "unsophisticated form" because of the spontaneity behind the wordscapes produced. They were process orientated; the writing of them being a therapeutic act, not necessarily having an end product–presentable poem as the objective.

Now, Nash and Poe are "good poets," too, despite employing the devices that I was becoming ambivalent about. I also sheepishly admit that I was unfamiliar with their works. With Stan's prompting I am quite excited about being able to relate to these two "poetic fathers'" styles. Though I did not copy them in any way previously, I am now motivated to learn from them, and maybe even come to enhance my rhyme, couplets, and repetition knowing now that these devices are "acceptable."

For those readers who are as unfamiliar as I was with Poe and Nash, I am including some brief examples of their work here. The first stanza of Poe's poem, "The Bells," (1995) follows:

Hear the sledges with the bells—
Silver bells!
What a world of merriment their melody foretells!
How they tinkle, tinkle, tinkle,
In the icy air of night!
While the stars that oversprinkle
All the Heavens, seem to twinkle
With a crystalline delight;
Keeping time, time, time,
In a sort of Runic rhyme,
To the tintinnabulation that so musically wells
From the bells, bells, bells, bells
Bells, bells, bells—
From the jingling and tinkling of the bells.

Stan drew my attention in this poem to the internal rhyme and significant repetition that he feels frames and orders my poetic form.

Two short poems of Nash's (1995), not only due to their rhymes and couplets, but subject matter too, are poems that I think I might have felt very comfortable writing myself:

Everybody Tells Me Everything

I find it very difficult to enthuse
Over the current news.
Just when you think that at least the outlook is so black that it can
grow no blacker, it worsens,
And that is why I do not like the news, because there has never
been an era when so many things were going so right for so
many of the wrong persons."

Celery

Celery, raw,
Develops the jaw,
But celery, stewed,
Is more quietly chewed.

Despite the validation that the styles of Poe and Nash give to my poetry's form, some critics of it have raised important points. Seeing that the couplet may provide a restrictive way to present my feelings and ideas, they note that on those occasions when I have departed from rhyme, deeper feelings may seem to be expressed. Though these critics do raise important points, as with visual art, the reader's/critic's projections onto another's written verse are significantly influenced by their own specific backgrounds and perspectives of the moment as well (Makin, 1994).

At the end of my doctoral programme, I attended a workshop on "Contemporary Poetry Writing" during which I became increasingly aware that as is the case with my spontaneously created art, my spontaneously created poetry follows no plan: whatever comes out and however it comes out is what makes up the final poem; editing and intentional structuring not being a part of my process. I found myself trying to explain to professional poets/writers and visual artists how and why I am not product-oriented–The minute I start to be conscious of why or how I want to break free from my rhyming couplets, there is a shift. The message that I am, unconsciously, trying to bring to the surface in words is affected somehow, and doesn't seem to flow the same way.

The rhyming/not rhyming debate in mind, I have come to realise latterly, that poems which feel "real" to me are in various styles. I guess, when I first started creating poems, I was influenced by my childhood education, that a poem was not a poem unless it rhymed. Then, as I finally became more "worldly," and the world seemed to become less conventionally-oriented, literally, and due to my own maturation and travels, I started to realise that could be moved on from old practices. So, my modest transition from rhyme: breaking childhood and adolescent programming, not just where it pertains to poetry, has not been a simple procedure. Accepting what comes out, if it is not in rhyme, instead of thinking that it is not poetry has caused interesting transformations in my ways of thinking generally It takes some order out of my life, and gives me license to get directly to the point, even if the point is not couched in the often protective humour and tentativeness of rhyme.

Rhyme, I have come to realise, has facilitated the promotion of much paradox for me. It has both helped me to be bold, and protected me from what I see as being too obvious. However, whether my wordscapes rhyme or are disjointed, what matters to me is beyond their form. That I feel connected to the insights and confirmations that they offer is of greater importance; that my wordscapes say what is paramount or hidden in my mind at the time of writing, providing me with relief, confirmations, or revelations. I also know that when my wordscapes strike a chord for me, it is more than likely that others will derive equally strong feelings from them. The deeply personal tending to be the strongly universal, the subtitle of this book is, appropriately, "*Revealing and Healing.*"

Overviewing the Wordscapes

As already noted, the individual sections and chapters in this book can be read sequentially or dipped into individually. Section One is entitled, "Relationships." These are demonstrated through our connections with other people and processes. Section Two is entitled, "Feelings." These describe emotions that emerge from the self and the self in relation, both difficult and easier ones. Section Three is entitled, "Activities." These are what can take us away from, interrupt, or affect our relationships and feelings; they are distractions and interactions. Section Four is entitled, " Natural Forces." These are what is there and what happens to us despite ourselves (our relationships, feelings, and/or activities), and involve the environment and the body.

In the individual chapters in Section One, the following themes are focused on: "Single," "Family," "Friends and Acquaintances," and "Community," under the heading, "People." "People" refers to individuals and groups that we are a part of or with whom we interact. "Single" considers some of the trials and tribulations of being alone, without an intimate partner as distinct from nuclear or extended family members. "Family" looks at some of the members of the nuclear family unit: their specific roles, incumbent intrigues, and expectations and benefits or otherwise. "Friends and Acquaintances" is concerned with those outside the family circle with whom we have particular connections or informal encounters, which may be intense, obligatory or superficial.

Under the heading, "Processes," what we go through and circumstances attached to our interactions with others are explored through the following themes: "Dating," "Breaking Up," "Abuse," and "Relocation." "Dating" is seen as a mechanism for developing possibilities for finding an intimate relationship with another. "Breaking

Up" considers when intimate relationships might not have worked, and dilemmas surrounding their endings. "Abuse" is viewed as an important reason to end a relationship; it can be seen to occur when advantage is taken of relationship privileges. "Relocation" looks at how moving to another place can highlight our need to fit in or for relationships.

In the individual chapters in Section Two, under the heading, "Difficult Times," the following themes are focused on: "Loss," "Loneliness," and "Depression." Difficult feelings are usually the ones that we do not want to have; not only are they unpleasant, but they also tend to linger longer and drive harder. "Loss" discusses when who or what we once had or were connected to is no longer there, unavailable, or gone forever. "Loneliness" describes that which is either caused by loss or the longing for what one does not have. "Depression" is seen to be reactive, as generated by loss and loneliness, or due to predisposing personality factors: sentiments from hopelessness and despair to, in the extreme, no longer having the desire to go on.

Under the heading, "Easier Times," those which everyone longs for, the preclusion of struggles offering or promising joy and happiness, is explored through the themes of "Hope/Relief," and "Love." "Hope/Relief" looks at what can lift us out of our difficult feeling states, excites our imaginations, and fuels our desires to go on. "Love" is seen to be a "highlight" of our easier times; (wo)man's ultimate comfort being to love and be loved.

In the individual chapters in Section Three, under the heading, "Distractions," the following themes are focused on: "Work," "Studies," "Vacation," and "Pastimes." "Distractions" refer to our obligations, responsibilities and relaxation opportunities that both give us routines and take us out of routines. Without "Work" we cannot sustain our families and may well not occupy our days, talents, interests or energies effectively. "Studies" provide opportunities for knowledge acquisition that could enable us to go further at work, play, or in our personal lives. "Vacation" looks at the effects of taking a break from routine (work, studies, or personal situations) for recharging and refreshing our energies. "Pastimes" discusses activities that may be performed on a daily basis when we are not able to take a vacation; it is good to have something to choose to focus our energies on that is different, particularly if it is creative.

Under the heading, "Interactions," what transpires between individuals with others or the world, who explain, redirect, or interrupt our course is explored through the themes of, "Challenges," and "Communications." "Challenges" looks at when our routines or habits come up against obstacles that are not easy or sure. "Communications" considers certain challenges that come our way which involve "communications issues" or when communications can be seen to be "interesting" in themselves.

In the individual chapters in Section Four, under the heading, "The Environment," the following themes are discussed: "Nature," "Weather," and "The Calendar." "The Environment" refers to settings, climates and time regulators outside of the body, that cause changes that are usually beyond our control. "Nature" considers elements in the settings around us that have lives of their own beyond human existence, that both cause us to wonder or are impediments. "Weather" describes climactic constancies or extremes that affect our daily lives and feeling states. "The Calendar" organizes our days, and gives us times of year and schedules: sometimes time works for us, and, at others, against us; occasionally we are "in sync."

Under the heading, "The Body," the concern is with what happens to it in the course of our development and growth, including that which is often beyond our control. The themes of "Health," "Illness," and "Aging" are discussed here. With respect to "Health," when we take care of it or it takes care of us, other things go more easily. "Illness" is viewed in the context of the exigencies of ill health; struggles and incumbent learning experiences often emerge. "Aging" is seen as a process that we have limited control over, and that is often accompanied by ill health: in the '90s the trend is to fight it wholeheartedly.

THE WORDSCAPES COLLECTION

Psychology would do better to turn directly to literature rather than to use it unaware.
(Ben Knights, 1995)

SECTION ONE: RELATIONSHIPS

RELATIONSHIPS refer to who we are as demonstrated by our connections with other people and processes, and their connections with us. According to Alan Roland (1988), in the East, personal needs for sociability, dependence, security, and status are fulfilled through strongly affective intimacy relationships in the extended family. In the West, the individual tries to fulfill those needs through friends and extra-familial social groups, society tending to be highly mobile and emotional ties more temporary. Therefore, intimate relationships in the United States are seen to be far more unstable and precarious than in India and Japan.

The two sections of poetry that follow consider two main components of relationships, the people who may be involved, and some processes that they may go through. They are "People" and "Processes."

A. People

People are individuals and groups that we are a part of or with whom we interact. It is as Barbara Streisand's popular song declared, people needing people are the luckiest people in the world. In considering people, the subsections that follow look at the individual as well as particular groups that individuals are usually members of and their respective dynamics. They are "Single," "Family," "Friends and Acquaintances," and "Community."

1. Single

Single refers to the trials and tribulations of being alone, without an intimate partner as distinct from family. Herbert Strean (1995) notes,

"Indices of interpersonal conflict and psychological stress are consistently higher among the unmarried."

The poems included here focus on stressors for singles: the events they attend, the longings and sadnesses they feel, and dynamics between singles and marrieds.

(1) Back On The "Singles Scene"

Two events, a party and a talk

I hate having to stalk!

They're not bad venues,
But it depends who's on the menus!

I'm sure that the "singles scene" hasn't changed,
But,
I have!

(2) Singles' Parties, Brunches And Weekends

Singles parties, brunches, and weekends,
Every day
Every week
Every month

If you want to put yourself through their paces,
You can go under the microscope of participants' leering faces

Easier ways to meet?...

Are there really any?

(3) At The Singles' Event

With noise and smoke, you've squashed and squeezed
With noise and smoke, you feel anxious and teased
"Singles' events," unconducive to civilized meetings

Ears buzzing, clothes smelling,
Head aching, grimaces telling

Distressing and humiliating,
Stressful and denigrating.

(4) At The Sushi Bar

At the sushi bar,
You have that flash

At the sushi bar,
It's no longer so rash

Sitting there with your mother is nice,
But, with another, you'd prefer to be breaking the ice

At the sushi bar,
You feel sad

At the sushi bar,
You know you ought to be glad

All these entertainments that you can afford,
No reason to feel bored

All these entertainments should put you in a better place,
So, why so much pain in your face?

Yet another awkward Saturday night,
Reminders of your dismal plight

Will "he" ever appear?
Will there ever be anyone to share what to you is dear?

(5) 36, 37, 38, 39, 40: Single Women In Their Prime

36,
Agony sticks

37,
Will you ever reach your heaven?

38,
You're running toward a closing gate

39,
How much longer can you say you're "fine?"

40,
A lost forté

No, it was not your fault
Yes, you did know how to vault

The wrinkles around their eyes,
Souvenirs of all their tries

The greying of their hair,
Evidence of massive care

Half-heartedly, to parties they go,
To witness how stuck they are, deep in their sorrow

With full heart, they tell their tales
And, feeling their pains, the listener pales

How to help them, what to do?

Only one person, the one who isn't there
Can make their dreams come true!

(6) If You Don't Have A Relationship

If you don't have a relationship,
You must have a religion, addiction or study interest,
Zest for something

If you don't have a relationship,
You mustn't be sad when the leaves are so beautiful,
By immersing yourself in nature you should feel more hopeful.

(7) People With Pushchairs

People with pushchairs parading down the street,
People with pushchairs rolling over your feet

Everywhere you turn, you can't escape their gaze,
Flaunting their precious infants, they seek your praise

And yes, you wish that you were there,
You've never known the other side of that stare

You know why you get so upset?
Because they've got what you want in their net.

(8) The Fight

Other people's babies,
Other people's lives

But her own...
Filled with "maybes,"
She who forever strives

Strives?
No!
Strived?
Yes!

And finally, she gives up the fight,
Throat feeling very tight

Heavy pain behind the eyes,
For help, looking up to the skies

And, guess what,
No one's there!

(9) If They Were Single

Would they be so happy if they were alone?
Would there ever be a day that they didn't moan?

Where do their airs of self-confidence really come from?
From being Mr. Dad and Mrs. Mom?

All the last minute plans that they make,
Not having to think who with them they might take

All the long-term arrangements that they realise,
Who will be around next year, not having to surmise

For them, life is relatively routine,
As a unit, they're known and seen

And, at the end of the day,
They have each other
Even if that other sometimes gets in the way

And, when they need a hug and boost,
Salvation is never very far
They go home to roost.

2. Family

The membership of a family unit and roles of specific members can offer intrigues, expectations, or benefits. Thomas Moore (1996) discusses family's value both on personal and social levels. He notes how being in a family elicits different reactions from outsiders than being single does. He discusses how when he travels with his wife and children, he is treated differently because people pay attention to his children. Moore (1996) also reflects on how the disappearance of family businesses and spread of impersonal, massive, anonymously owned and operated stores has "sucked the soul from everyday life."

The poems included here focus on the effects of aging on the parent-child relationship, mother's influence, sibling issues, and unconditional love.

(1) Aging Parents

Parents age
What will happen next on their stage?

Masters at stirring up guilt,
You succumb,
Worrying that they'll wilt

Parents age,
No sooner out of their cage than back in!

Freedom will be short,
If you listen to their every retort

...Parent to child,
Child to parent...

A vicious circle of responsibility
With little place for humility

Not knowing when and how to take a stand,
Your interactions cannot be planned

No, you're not in command!

(2) Parents Of Grown-Up Children

Do they ever view you as an adult?
Not behaving themselves as adults

Each visit,
It's you that has to put on the show

Each visit,
Your deeper feelings they desire not to know

It's their way or no way,
They live in a fantasy

It's their way or no way,
They deny your reality

That they will reconcile their world with yours,
Impossible!

For upsets,
You're the one responsible!

(3) In Distance To Touch

Mother's advice,
Always nice

Mother's ear,
Always near

Miles apart,
Difficult to impart

In distance to touch,
Means so much.

(4) Mother's Voice

Mother's voice inside of me

Telling me,
Warning me,
Imploring me

Mother's voice always there

Taking a large share,
Giving a feeling of care,
Attentive beyond compare.

(5) My Mother's Face

My mother's face, I saw it in the mirror today

Looking me straight in the eyes,
Her knowing came right my way

Even when being me, I hold her inside,
Even when far apart, her expressions within me hide

A flash across my face,
Memory takes place

Am I in conflict with who she is, was, and can be?
Or, is there a narrowing of differences between her and me?

That she sees me in her, I have some doubt,
If she tried to be more like me, her life would be caused to turn about

What's happening?

Is she more accepting of my individuality?
Or,
Are we actually reaching some parity?

(6) A Sibling

A sibling,
Always quibbling
Of the same flesh and blood,
But more often than not, treats you like mud

And then, the happy day arrives,
When he realises that there is a connection between your lives
Whatever niceties he offers,
Take!

Even if confused at his change of heart
Accept it!
Let something start

(7) How Well Do You Know Your Brother?

Your brother,
How long has it been?

The last time you lived at home he was barely a teen

And then, the years went by,
On visits he'd hardly give you a "hi!"

The looks of pain behind his face,
Did you really know what happened over time in his space?

Questions without answers, you gave up soon,
He looked at you like a creature from the moon

No matter how hard you tried,
In the end,
By yourself, you cried

The mystery of those missing years,
The information gaps about his cares

Time in some cases can make things better,
But, in this one, it's been hard to communicate

Even a letter.

(8) Thank You

Thank you for your care, despite all,
Thank you for picking me up when I fall

Thank you for listening, not condoning,
Thank you for being there, always phoning.

3. Friends and Acquaintances

Friends and acquaintances are those people outside the family circle with whom we have particular connections or informal encounters which can be intense, obligatory or superficial. As Marjorie and Michael Rutter (1993) state, "Intense relationships (whether between close friends, lovers, or parents and children) tend to have exclusive qualities....Also, the desire for close relationships is an important part of most people's biological makeup, so that when one relationship is failing, compensation may be sought in some other relationship."

The poems included here focus on both the better and less pleasant aspects of friendship, long-distance correspondence between friends, and influences on and of acquaintances.

(1) Friends

Friends, so dear
But, what to do when they're not near?

When friends are good
How sorely they're missed

Replacements,
Can't just make them exist

When friends are good,
How sorely they're missed

(2) A Good Friend

A good friend,
Sharer of anxieties

Someone who is bothered about you,
Willing to bend
Someone to open up to,
A listening ear will extend

Caring questions,
Heartening discretions

Some qualities of a good friend

(3) A Letter From An Old Friend

How do you really know what's going on in someone's head?
After all they've done, the spoken and the unsaid

You feel quite ignored

So, breathe a sigh,
They may well have been busy or shy

Your convictions, though strong,
Could just be proven wrong

Then, out of the blue,
They contact you

Justify their delay,
And, for communication, open a gateway

But, how do you know if this is friendship seeking to reconnect?
After so many months and feelings of rejection and neglect.

(4) Mail To Over The Sea

To my good friends over the sea,

I wish that you were nearer,
That we could do a movie and dinner,
Gossip about "nothing" on the 'phone

When you were in town, I never felt so alone

Please keep filling me in on all your news,
It's nice about your letters to enthuse

Don't think I'm crazy,
Don't think I'm lazy

You can, if you wish, ignore my mood,
But with you, I know, that I can be sincere,
Not hide how I brood

(5) Sharing Misery With A Girlfriend

Sharing misery with a girlfriend,
But does it help?

Sharing misery with a girlfriend,
But how many more times?

Together you both sigh,
"Alas! Not one nice guy!"

(6) Betrayed By A Friend

Friendship, friendship

What is a good friend?
Where do friendships start, and how do they end?

With boundaries, divisions, secrets,
Intimacy becomes restricted,
Friendship feels constricted

With issues of trust and affairs of the heart,
Loyalties can be torn apart

Changing motivations,
Lead to new relations

Kindnesses extended,
Mustn't be one-ended

When your inside lets you know—no!
Take those feelings and go!

(7) A Better Option

Arrangements made,
Time put aside

Then, a ring of the 'phone
You're on your own

Someone else was free...

A better option,
Forgotten me.

(8) Excuse Me

An emotional state that's not great

Aches, pains
Those feelings that are stronger than can be put into words
Not feeling very safe, in control or sure
With injuries to body and mind that have taken their toll

Energy very depleted
Struggling not to be defeated

In reflective mood
And tired of reflecting

But, every time I stop,
The tears appear

My racing heart takes its own reprieve

So, if I'm not always there,
Excuse me

It's not you, just something I'm going through

Being able to do what comes next,
Putting my life back into context.

(9) The Advice Of Others

Others' advice can be nice,
But, by taking it, you tread on thin ice

Others advice may be what you need at the minute,
But, outsiders never really feel what it's like to be in it!

Others advice is usually given with good intent,
Their objectivity, however, is often bent

Regrets at a later stage are no compensation,
Others' advice not always guaranteeing satisfaction.

(10) To My Hairdresser

That timely chat,
Putting in place where life's at

That consistent smile,
Letting you know that you're worthwhile

A counsellor and friend,
She's listened to every one of your stories to the end!

4. Community

"Community" is made up from the wider circle of people where we live, work, study or play: those with whom we often have more formal and less spontaneous relationships but who may satisfy a purpose or need that we have. Moore (1996) considers an idealistic community that discovers "the sheer joy of creating a way of life that serves families, ennobles work, and fosters genuine communal spirit."

The poems included here consider both advantages and disadvantages of community membership, the comforts it affords as well as the difficulties adhesion often involves.

(1) Sense Of Community

Sense of community,
Increased immunity

Increased immunity from colds, headaches, and loneliness,
Increased immunity from pain, anxiety, and hopelessness

In distance to touch,
That means so much

At proximity to hold,
Joy's allowed to unfold

Solitude,
At times necessary,
But not always beneficial

Quietude,
At times necessary,
But not always crucial

Community,
Giver of comfort and reassurance,
Challenges can also induce

Community,
Making life less of an endurance,
Peace of mind, can also produce.

(2) The Group

I love leading this group,
Being part of the "troop"

It makes me feel whole,
In control

Worthwhile,
Able to smile

Strong,
Because I belong.

(3) Others

Conversation,
Identification

Thoughts of others,
Quite familiar
Views of others,
Not dissimilar

Discussion,
Elucidation

Lives of others,
Taking similar course
Hopes of others,
Indicating competitive force

Clarification,
Confirmation.

(4) Fuller Heart

Fuller heart,
Quietened mind

Alas for the depart,
People here have been so very kind

Though I can spend time alone,
they don't allow me to spend time in my head,
Every night I sleep better in my bed

Life once again becomes worth living,
There's a mutual sense of giving

And, it seems, I don't have to do much,
No matter my face, they give me that gentle touch

Honest care and concern,
Not even something that I've had to earn
They like me for being me,
No sense of hostility

They're open back,
No feeling of attack

Whatever I do or say
Things seem to go the right way.

(5) Temporary Reprieve

Temporary reprieve,
Yes, temporary

Because when this gathering is over,
You'll be alone again

Alone without supports,
Alone with a familiar deluge of troubling thoughts

No distractions

Hostile environment

Triggers for discontent

No matter how soothed you've been
Loved and cared for you've felt
The external aids bestowed momentarily cannot be enough

Permanency of favourable environment is what you seek

No matter how prepared you are within yourself
You, yourself, alone, can no longer do it

Temporary reprieve
Is not what you want

Involvement, partnership, belonging, purpose
Is now the only thing that will make life livable
Nothing else is even remotely acceptable.

(6) A Good Sport

I'm tired of being a "good sport"
Going along with others' rules, conventions, ways

I'll fit in, yes, I'll fit in
But, will that help me win?

At work, at play
Do I ever get the final say, my own way

Or, do I just acquiesce,
Try to alleviate others' stress

I'm tired of being a "good sport"
Going along with others' rules, conventions, ways

Is it me who doesn't measure up?
Or do others not know when to "shut up?"

Like all others I have my faults, fears and dreads
But, maybe at night, they sleep better in their beds

Like all others, I need affirmation,
From everyday contacts, to receive less negation

I'll fit in, yes I'll fit in
But, will that help me win?

(7) The Party

Party starting...

About being invited,
Delighted and excited

People to meet,
An end to those hours of retreat

Party happening...

But not as expected,
Feeling superficially rejected

Party ending...

Head swimming,
Disappointment mounting

Deflation rules,
An evening with fools!

B. PROCESSES

Processes are what we go through or circumstances attached to our interactions with others. According to André Rae (1992), "Women are more likely to admit to themselves and to others the sadness, anger, or fear that they feel when they are alone. Men keep their feelings to themselves and, therefore, often fail to deal with them."

In considering processes, the subsections that follow look at some of the more common exchanges and circumstances that most of us experience at particular points in our lives. They are "Dating," "Breaking Up," and "Abuse."

1. Dating

Dating is a way to develop possibilities for finding an intimate relationship with another. While dating, heterosexual and otherwise, is important to both sexes, Rae (1992) considers how "during their lives, women develop more interpersonal skills than do men." With respect to men, she states, "From childhood onward, men are oriented to seeing their world in terms of achievement, while women see their world in terms of relationships."

The poems included here look at dating at various stages, particular behaviours associated with it, and gender specific issues and patterns.

(1) Dating Behaviour

There's dating behaviour
And regular behaviour

To their regular friends,
They're the "nicest guys"

But, to a blind date,
They can be the worst surprise

A whole other persona is shown,
Which can cause the most tolerant of females to moan

For men on dates,
There's seldom healthy states

With maturity offering no guarantees,
There are some real grand masters of tease

The stories that they tell,
Yes, they think they're swell

The return 'phone calls that they don't make,
A certain cause of heart-break

The emotional tax that they bill,
Cause for many a female ill

But, if the female seems to brood
She's the one considered rude

There's dating behaviour
And, there's regular behaviour.

(2) A New Relationship

Consideration, sensation, elation
Forming a healthy relation

The gentleness of his touch
His words that mean so much

That softness in his face,
So comforting to be in his space

Encounters of a new kind,
But old wounds are not always left behind

Although his words are sweet,
Do you really know his regular beat?

Although his alibis sound fine,
Why do you worry if he's giving you a line?

Have you met your match?
You're falling, but will he catch?

Wanting to be in his arms,
Wanting to feel his charms

Regretting the night without him near,
What did you fear?

How long do we have to wait?
Wanting that feeling of a more secure state.

(3) Staying With My Feelings

That I stay with those feelings I'm going to try,
I don't want my life to pass me by

That I feel for you, I can't deny
And you, you're not so shy

To continue on in "attraction mode," I'll endeavour
Never say "never!"

More time with you, I want to spend
Become a good friend

With more intimacy, hopefully, you'll realise our bond,
Become consciously connected to this open-armed blonde.

(4) The Types That I Attract

Wherever I turn, they draw near...
"Hang out with me for a while, have no fear!"

Whatever interests me, they claim an interest in too...
"We can do it together, just me and you!"

Then I attach, give them "all of me,"
They dance around with glee

Then they back away,
Say that they never had any intention to stay!

(5) Settle For A Nerd

With time ahead,
You don't listen to what people have said

But when you're getting on in age,
You're at a new stage
Your needs and values change fast

So he's not outrageously charming,
Why should that be alarming?

So he's not taking leaps with his career,
What have you to fear?

Reliable,
Available,
Acceptable

When you know what to expect, you can breathe a sigh,
Despite others' petty gossip he's a really "nice guy!"

(6) The "Other Woman"

Who to trust?
When to know not to go on...

Who to pursue with lust?
When to know not to go on...

Who to look at with disgust?
When to know not to go on...

Who to consider a must?
When to know not to go on...

Though the chemistry may be there,
Is it "safe" to get beyond that initial "stare?"

Married, divorced, cohabiting, transitioning,
Men, all so good at convincing gesturing

The "other woman" in someone's life you don't want to be,
Being an easy replacement or repository offers no security!
As someone else's "secret distraction,"
You'll receive no part of the "action"!

(7) Men Won't Understand

That your disinterest wasn't meant to devastate,
Men don't understand

That your disinterest wasn't meant to alienate,
Men don't understand

Difficult for them to be intimate,
Every explanation is taken as a threat

Difficult for them to accept defeat,
Men prefer their mates to come packaged up neat.

(8) A Younger Man

Younger in age,
But not in stage

Younger at heart,
Anyone can be your counterpart

Younger in age,
But he's entered your cage

Younger at heart,
A shared journey can still start

A connection is there,
So put aside your heavy care

A connection to nurture and love,
Accept the intrigue of this gentle dove

Fear not the gossip and the stares,
That others ever know the magnitude of your cares

Climb those unfamiliar stairs with ease,
You and he, each other, are the only ones to please

(9) The "Fix Up"

They'll fix you up, they say...
Hopefully,
But when?

The 'phone may ring one day,
But till then...

You don't want to show your anxiousness
Especially when they're at home together,
In their coziness

But, how long must you wait?
Endure this nervous state

You,
You sit by the 'phone

You,
You're all alone...

Your married friends quickly forget the grief of their single days,
Absorbed with themselves now, they have different ways

There's no rush to get you that date,
What the hell if you have to wait!

Of course, it's not such a big deal!

Don't let them think that you're so desperate,
From yours, their lives now, are so separate...

2. Breaking Up

When an intimate relationship doesn't work it may be necessary to
end it. According to Daniel Goleman (1995), an "early warning sign"
of a marriage being in danger is "harsh criticism." He states, "In a
healthy marriage husband and wife feel free to voice a complaint. But
too often in the heat of anger complaints are expressed in a destruc-
tive fashion, as an attack on the spouse's character." From another perspective, Joseph Nowinski (1993) discusses how the initial attraction
that draws two people together can sustain a relationship early on, but
explains how if intimacy fails to develop "that relationship will eventually either break up or slowly decline into a state of mutual alien-
ation."

The poems included here look at various stages of breaking up,
from recognition and procrastination, to resolution, pain, and ultimately possibilities for new growth.

(1) Feelings Not Mutual

The telephone rings,
A voice with expectation sings

Mutual feelings not present

Not even causing a smile,
Suggestions that start to sound futile

Time to be cruel but kind,
Others' emotions tending to be blind

Putting an end to the pursuit,
Poor other wasn't even en route

Assuming propriety must be ended,
Well-being and independence strongly defended

(2) Your Complicity

Insincerity, I won't handle it any more
Your games of platitude, I totally abhor!

Putting a show on for other people, I will not do,
I need to see authenticity, the real me, and the real you!

Theory's not enough,
The reality must be there

The reality may be tough,
But it's part of my heavy care

No, the game, I will not play,
Sadder and more alone, I may be at the end of the day

No, the game I will not play,
"Peace" I'm not making, just so that you'll have your way

When I'm not genuine, it doesn't sit right with me
You refuse to see what's really happening,
I can't accept your complicity!

(3) Waiting Laundry

What is "enough" anyway?

To move on or to stay?

Which alternative is the one that's bad?
What will make me mad?
What will make me glad?
A perpetual quandary,
Waiting laundry

An unpleasant situation,
Rising irritation.

(4) Saying Goodbye

I find it hard to say goodbye!

A big sigh!
The time is nigh
Having to be strong,
Knowing it won't take long

Not with happiness or glee,
But we know, in the long run, it's the best thing,
Both for you and for me

Thinking always to hold a place for you in my heart,
That feelings will never completely part

(5) Ending It

Do I want to end it?

Can I?

Will I?

Big sigh!

There's "something" there,
I think!?

For a life together, however, not enough
Time to be tough.

(6) The End

What a weekend,
What an end!

He, so much, wants to be my boyfriend,
No end!

Confusion,
Contusion,
Elusion,
Delusion

How long are we going to play this game?
Things are not the same

He's no dummy,
Maybe just too attached to mummy

Although he instinctively knows where things are at,
He continues to bat

He really thinks he loves me,
Hugs me
Tries to keep me in his control,
So that he can feel whole

Of his life, I'm one of the biggest parts,
Other interests only receiving tentative starts

No, I'm not what he needs...
Can't grow his seeds!

(7) The Pain

You came back into my life
Causing me strife

I'd told you, "Get a life!"

Now that you're near,
The pain starts to reappear

Can't live with you,
Can't be without you

Though I'm on the hunt,
There's no one else on the man front!

(8) Move On

Let me move on
Dare to grow
BE.

3. Abuse

Abuse can be an important reason for ending a relationship, often happening when relationship privileges are taken advantage of. Strean (1995) discusses "the emphasis on narcissism and hedonism in our culture," and its effects on marital interaction. "When individuals want instant gratification, they become angry and exasperated when their marital partners do not gratify their omnipotent and narcissistic yearnings." He notes that irrespective of who the aggressor might be, research indicates more people being likely to be "killed, physically assaulted, beaten up, slapped or spanked in their own homes more than anywhere else." He refers to Gelles who proposed, in 1972, that violence in the family is more common than love.

The poems included here consider forms, effects, and outcomes of abuse.

(1) Silence

You didn't want to speak to me today
Do I deserve it?

Maybe it's your way to attack,
Get me back

You see everything from your side,
But that makes me, my feelings hide

However, that's not the real issue between me and you,
About the long-term I'm concerned, what we do?

Put-downs, criticisms, disdain,
Moulding another person only causes pain

Signals from the inside,
My unconscious advises

Where's your sense of pride?

(2) The Abuser Wins

Why do abusers always win?

How do they face their abused with a wide-eyed grin?

And when his abuse has been done with you
He has a whole long list of others that is very new

Women will date him anytime, anywhere
About finding a husband is all they care

Women will warm to his charm,
Never seeing how he squeezed your arm

"Poor me!" he will bemoan,
Claiming that he himself was a "victim," and now is all alone

Would it be so easy for the abused!
By other men, they feel continually "used"

With no safe haven of a relationship that's good,
The difficulty they have getting back on their feet is never really understood.

(3) Without Respect Or Consideration

Cheat, liar, rogue
Without respect or consideration
You live your life.

(4) Only You

No, I did nothing wrong,
Only you

No "should have done differentlies,"
Only you

(5) Memories

On the edge of tears
Memories of you live on
Not good memories,
Painful moments.

(6) Self

Self, self
I'm back to self

Must not devalue self

Painful patterns repeated
Energy levels depleted

Attention to what's best for me
That which will foster my sanity

With a body that aches,
High stakes

My future is on the line
Yes

Not just his,
MINE!

4. Relocation

Moving to another place may highlight our need to fit in or form relationships. According to Robert Bly et al. (1993), "We don't so much build communities as we are already built into them. Just by being in the world our life is with others." So, when we change our location (the piece of the world in which our life is lived) we have to adjust to a different position in a new community that may be structured in a way with which we are not familiar.

The poems included here focus on the more alienating aspects of acculturation, only alluding to the enchantment cultural variance can hold.

(1) Cultural Difference

You changed countries

So what?
A racial minority you're not!

You moved countries

So adapt!
What happened?—You napped?

Only now, with the passage of time, have you realized...
The scars of the ostracised

Childhood in other parts
Had prepared you for different outcomes,
More certain starts

Childhood away
Made life abroad no easy play!

(2) Language Barrier, Cultural Variance

Language barrier

Patience builds competence,
Being understood enhances confidence

Cultural variance an enchantment

(3) L'Etranger

Outsider, outcast, "étranger,"
Loner, "objet d'intrigue," not here to stay

Attend their meeting,
Be a good sport

Make your visit fleeting,
Hold back all retort!

(4) No Roots

Natives are always nice when it suits,
You accommodate to establish roots

Natives will manipulate and cajole,
And...
With no one for your console,
Exploitation takes its toll

You lose!
It's your heart they stole!

(5) Sunday In A New Town

A sense of hopelessness, feelings of loss,
No one to comfort or even boss
Hours to sit alone, brood...
To get up or stay in bed?
A move of the head, it feels like lead

Disinterest of a community,
How does an outsider break their spell,
Be accepted well?

With dear ones lacking,
The desire to "get packing"

Bad timing, mal à l'aise, discontent

Hours pass
And finally...
The day is "spent"!

Lack of activity,
A feeling of rigidity

Tension mounts,
Human contact counts!

Stress turns a dangerous bend,
No one to talk it out
In need of a friend

No ringing telephone,
The reality of being alone
Neither laughter nor argument,
Fighting self-pity and depression with lament!

SECTION TWO: FEELINGS

Feelings are emotions that emerge from the self or in relation to outside stimuli (people, situations, and the environment) that promote both difficult and easier times. The premise of Goleman's book *Emotional Intelligence* (1995) is that people who are emotionally adept have an advantage. The emotionally adept not only know and manage their own feelings well, but read and deal effectively with other peoples' feelings, whether in romance and intimate relationships or in grasping the unspoken rules that ensure success in organizational politics.

The two sections of poetry that follow consider two main types of feelings, those experienced with difficulty and those experienced with ease. They are "Difficult Times" and "Easier Times."

A. Difficult Times

Difficult times are what we usually don't want to have happen. Not only are difficult feelings unpleasant, but they also tend to linger longer and drive harder. Goleman (1995) describes a main function of sadness as being to help in adjustment to significant losses or disappointments. He states, "Sadness brings a drop in energy and enthusiasm for life's activities, particularly diversions and pleasures, and, as it deepens and approaches depression slows the body's metabolism." He describes how this "introspective withdrawal" creates the opportunity not only for being able to mourn a loss or frustrated hope, but also to understand the consequences that it might have for one's life. Then, as energy returns, new beginnings can be planned. "This loss of energy may well have kept saddened–and vulnerable–early humans close to home, where they were safer."

104

In considering difficult times, the subsections that follow look at three main feeling states that although significant individually, can also follow on sequentially from one another: "Loss," "Loneliness," "Depression."

1. Loss

Loss happens when who or what we once had or were connected to may no longer be available, or is gone forever. The premise of Ian Craib's book, *The Importance of Disappointment* (1994), is that social developments, both from the near and distant past, have contributed to a society which tends to deny disappointment and its necessity. Craib points out how disappointment arises even in situations which might be associated with the generation of more positive reactions, such as having a baby, getting married, and being promoted at work. These often bring about unexpected feelings of loss and depression, which he describes as appropriate in many cases being that they entail "the loss of situations and relationships that will never return."

The poems included here consider feelings activated by loss and particular losses: coping mechanisms and challenges to them, as well as possibilities for new growth.

(1) Loss

That empty feeling inside,
Distraction that you can't hide
That you didn't take enough care,
Self-criticism is hard to bear

That it would be appreciated more if it would reappear,
Now I know how much it was really dear!

(2) Numbed Feelings

Numb those feelings,
Deny them

Numb those feelings,
What's the point of them anyway?

To others
They have no point

But to you
The pain they provide is unbelievable

For others
They don't understand why you stick with them

But to you
The alternatives imaginable don't appear

There are no alternatives
No other options
No changes

Everything's the same
The same, but worse

Why?
Because you've been through these times before

Before
And before
And before

Despite all your endeavours,
No more! You wish

Despite all your precautions,
No more! You hope

But, there's no way out,
No fresh pastures

So, you function on automatic pilot,
Don't bother anyone

They don't like to see how you really feel,
They don't want to hear your rumblings any more

Then, when you hold everything in,
There's added punishment

When you smile,
You make the others around you feel better

But, with numbed feelings,
How long can you live?

With numbed feelings
The barely satisfied self wilts

With numbed feelings
Life loses reason

Enter the "blah"

Numbed feelings
Meaningfulness gone

A challenge to carry on

With numbed feelings

(3) No Thoughts Of You

Without thoughts of you,
I feel somewhat blue

But, with thoughts of you,
Nothing may come true

Needing you to validate my feelings,
Because, alone, there's no dealings

Need you to give me the "all clear"

To have "warm fuzzies"
Without fear!

(4) A Piece Of My Heart

A piece of my heart that's no longer mine,
Whine after whine

And you're okay,
Take no responsibility for my pain

And you're okay,
Can't bear to hear me complain

Then time moves on by,
You become more adept at being shy

Willing me to back off, you make contact with me a duty,
Getting on with your own life, you've carried away your booty!

A piece of my heart was bitten away,
Day by day.

(5) Paper And Time

So much wasted paper
All on you

So many painful thoughts
All on you

Time for myself
Wasted

Paper and time,
Not to be filled again.

(6) On The Edge Of Tears

On the edge of tears
All the time

On the edge of tears
Held back for others
On the edge of tears
They'll only take a minute

On the edge of tears

Ironically,
Someone else should be doing the crying

(7) On A Whim

On a whim,

I think I can be strong
But, for how long?

Soon, I'm taken over

Feeling like I'm out on a limb,
I ask myself, "How can I manage without him?"

I only wanted things to work

And now, I find I'm waning
The emotional expenditure has been draining.

(8) Human Ecstasy Preferred

Spending the evening with you,
Made me forget all the work I have to do

Spending the evening with you,
Today, makes me feel somewhat blue
Getting back on track, I've had a hard job,
On the edge of a sob

To convince myself that these studies are worth it,
Now, I find it hard to admit

In a relationship, I'd rather be,
Experiencing some human ecstasy
In my books, I find it hard to stay,
Dissatisfied, I am, living my life this way

And to the outside world, I may appear smart,
But, within me I know I'd be a lot happier with a compatible heart!

How to get to there from here,
I no longer know

How to get to there from here,
I'm impatient to go!

(9) Burn Out

The forest burns to replenish

Thyroid, chronic fatigue, allergies
Pills, injections, doctors' appointments

Alternatives...

Cancelling enjoyed activities
Restricting foods
Walking around in a daze

Solitude...

Frustration compounds anger
Anger compounds pain

Walking around in a daze
That long wait for better days

Remembering how it used to feel
Wanting a life again that's real

To quit explaining to others that
You can't help it
To cherish what you have
More dearly

Because you lost it—
Nearly

The forest will grow afresh.

2. Loneliness

Loneliness may well be caused either by loss or the longing for what one does not have. Goleman (1995) states the following:

Add the sounds of silence to the list of emotional risks to health—and close emotional ties to the list of protective factors. Studies done over two decades involving more than thirty-seven thousand people show that social isolation—the sense that you have nobody with whom you can share your private feelings or have close contact—doubles the chances of sickness or death.

The poems included here consider the nature of loneliness and mechanisms that promote its manifestation; particularly those that are socially driven and create unfortunate impasses for the lonely person. Sometimes we wonder if anyone notices us at all, if others would feel things were different without us there.

(1) Loneliness

Solo, lost,
Forlorn, tossed

Isolation and introversion,
Diminished assertion

Lacking usefulness,
Forgetting thankfulness

Pounding Loneliness.

(2) A Lot Of Lonely People

There's a lot of lonely people out there,
All wanting to say hello

Pretending not to have a care,
Wishing to get up and go

Desiring to share.

(3) Dreaded Silence

Silence,
Dreaded silence
Blinding, deafening silence

Praying for abatement,
Even a ring of the 'phone, for a mini-curtailment

Silence,
Empty and pounding
No one interrupting, nothing resounding

Well and truly on your own,
Privacy suffers no infringement when you're all alone

Silence,
Dreaded silence,
Blinding deafening silence

Ice-cold, unending, cruel silence!

(4) The Concert

I wanted to go to the concert tonight,
Had the tickets in sight

But, with no one to ask
Scheming to find someone became a real task

I wanted to go to the concert tonight,
Had the tickets in sight

But with activities I can do alone,
I have my limitations

How long must I wait for others to offer invitations?

(5) Demonstrative In Public

Demonstrative in public,
You wish they wouldn't

Demonstrative in public,
But, you too, have done things you shouldn't

In love,
You want to tell the world

Alone,
In a fetal ball, you remain curled

Others' open gestures you question,
Are they really happy behind their pretension?

Others' open exhibitions you envy,
Will you ever, again, experience that ecstasy?

(6) Every Day Intimacy

Focusing on the day,
Letting that get in the way

The wider picture seems to have no place,
You feel the pain across your face!

Travel plans, projects in mid-stream,
They make you want to scream!

Alone is not a good place to be,
Impedes your sanity!

Alone, you seem to forget
Can't celebrate about any project

That's not what matters in the "here and now"
What you really need is a daily "wow"!

A hug from someone dear,
A friendly, listening ear

Someone to come home to at night,
With whom, from the world, you can take flight

Every day intimacy!

(7) Long-Distance Correspondence

Letters in the mail are received with joy,
Letters in the mail can make your day

But, in between, you're all alone,
On your own, you have time to moan

Letters in the mail, are received with joy,
Letters in the mail can make your day

But, in between, you miss the physical connection,
On your own, too much time for introspection.

(8) Survival

Alone again,
The head pounding

Alone again,
Too many thoughts resounding

Disciplined and occupied,
Defended and reserved,
Controlled and protected

The key to survival

A mastery of the self,
No rival.

(9) On Being Alone: No Key

To have someone hold me and really mean it,
To have someone hold me and really feel it

How would that be?
Could that ever be?

Couples in the street, what's behind their hold?
Couples in the street, their true feelings have they ever told?

And so the longing continues without abate,
And so the days go by, not one satisfactory date

The emptiness is so hard to bear,
My heart swells, filled with heavy care

Mistress of my own destiny, I may be,
But, where an intimate partner is concerned, no key

(10) The Power Of One

The power of one,
Power?
No power
To a table at the back, you're shown
Waiters and clientele alike, know you're all alone

Looks of pity, wonder, disdain
All by herself, some "plain Jane!"

(11) Lunchtime Poem

Back out into the world
You surfaced for lunch

Back out into the world
It was a regular Monday noon

Office workers
Scurried for a quick bite

Delivery trucks
Made curbside calls

Squirrels weaved their way
Through the bank of decorative foliage

Open buds
Stood back and watched

Sounds of engines interrupted
Smells of stifled, recycled air

Sensitive ears and nostrils felt
Quite oppressed

A restlessness
A feeling of uncertainty
Glints of excitement

Each competed for a spot

You reentered the world
Wondered about your place
Did anyone notice that you were

Back
Could make a difference
By your mere presence...or absence
Had something to say

Would you carve your way
Or, be oppressed by forces around

Did anything change while you weren't there?
Will your life be different now
Because of this interlude?

3. Depression

Depression can be reactive, possibly generated by loss and loneliness, or due to predisposing personality factors: Sentiments range from hopelessness and despair, to, in the extreme, no longer having the desire to continue.

Goleman (1995) discusses how women, rather than men, are far more prone to ruminate when they are depressed; women, in fact, are diagnosed with depression twice as often as men. Referring to Nolen-Hoeksma's findings, Goleman mentions other significant factors. Women, for instance, are both more open to disclosing their distress and have more in their lives to be depressed about. Men, however, may drown their depression in alcoholism, their drinking rate being about twice as much as that of women.

The poems included here look at depression from the inside out, through various stages, symptoms, and mind-sets of the depressive cycle. When disappointments threaten energies for life, the situation is serious, since voids risk never being filled. Only the last poem hints at relief.

(1) Life's Better In My Dreams

Bed, Bed,
Sanctuary for my head
Bed, Bed,
Where all I wish for can get said

As I drift into a feature film with the one I pine for,
As I have adventure after adventure with someone who wants me more and
more

Everything seems to work with greater satisfaction than in real life,
No upsets or strife!

I finally get what I want, relax, have a moment of calm,
And then it's time for the "wake-up" alarm...

Waking up, I put it on hold,
Go back under the sheets, pushing away reality's cold

For a few moments more, I drift,
My days of gliding give, in real time, only thirty seconds more lift

No more picnics in the sun,
Days of endless fun

No more candle lit dinners,
With dates who are genuine winners

Wrestling not to wake,
I put everything at stake!

Without punishment-free over-indulgence, I'm back to being blue,
What's the point of having my cake when I can't eat it too?

Back to the kind of snow that doesn't melt when on it you tread,
Back to negotiating downtown streets with dread

Real life, so familiar with its prohibitions!
Real life, never boring, an inventory of conditions!

(2) Bed Too Late

Unproductive reflection

Self-negating,
Creator of rejection

In the morning, strong warning,
Headache dawning, painful yawning

Better to sleep,
Shut-eyed benefits to reap

Wiser to forget,
Staying up enhances regret

Bed too late,
This folly must end

To drift, thinking, idle, not a healthy state.

(3) Sanctuary

Security in bed,
Sanctuary for the head

Away from the world
Body snuggled and curled

Not wanting to get up, move
Dreams and dazes increase, improve

Can't face the day,
Want to keep reality at bay

Telephone, please don't sound,
I don't want to be found

Needing time to forget all, to rest
Regenerate motivations, in sleep invest

(4) To Go To Bed Not To Sleep

To go to bed
Not to sleep

Weeping your way through the night,
Gently

Gently,
That others don't see

On the morn'
Your disequilibrated state.

(5) The Troubled Mind

The troubled mind troubles on,
And, when the day is done
The troubled mind troubles on

The troubled mind troubles on,
And, when the night comes
The troubled mind troubles on

No rest, no solace, no refreshment

How?

Nothing soothes, nothing reassures, nothing replaces

The troubled mind troubles on

(6) Things Could Be Worse

No dear,
Things could be worse

It's not cancer, AIDS, or divorce

And, there's money in your purse

...No dear

I think it's because there's nothing really wrong,
That you can't get along

Another damp pillow-case,
Another disrupted night's sleep

No one to call out to when your mind begins to race,
No one to look in on you, even a peep

Alone in your bed of tears,
Alone with all your fears

Heartache and pain oozing from your face,
This time, no makeup can hide their trace

Being sorry and sad doesn't help,
But neither does it to give a yelp

(7) Intervention In Destiny

An unknown place,
Treading lightly

An expressionless face,
Moving hesitantly

An aura of calm,
A meditative state

Bereft of charm,
A widened gait

To get to there from here,
Foreboding and fear
An uncertain destination,
Encourager of much procrastination

Mind quietening,
The jingling in the ears ends

Clearer about what can be frightening,
The message that it sends

On a journey going nowhere, you're suspended in time,
When, on a journey going somewhere, you'd prefer to be

Intervention not a choice

Destiny.

(8) Hope

Hell
On
Planet
Earth

(9) Those Deep Blue Waters Beckon You Near

Slipping over the edge,
For so many months, you walked that narrow ledge

From hyperactivity to depression,
From total fatigue to fruitless aggression

And now, you feel like you're nearly there again,
Your face taking on those feelings of pain

Your heart pounding its beat of lament,
How are the next few months going to be spent?

You must lift yourself out,
Hold off another painful bout

Those deep blue waters beckon you near,
You sleep fitfully, managing your fear

The abyss is there facing you, right ahead,
Months of isolation in a tearful bed

Is this what you want or need right now?
No!
You have to gain control, move on somehow!

(10) My Live Spirit

My live spirit roamed many mountains
My live spirit sailed many seas

Then,
A consequence of all this wandering.
My live spirit was weakened,
Softened,
Quietened,
Hibernated

Disappointment set in

With this, the ability to risk any action
Thought
Response
Was gone

The space where my spirit lived was vacated
Longing unsatiated.

(11) It's The Small Things

It's the small things,
Like sitting out in the sun for an hour
That gives you back your power

It's the small things,
Like taking some time out to have lunch
That about how life's supposed to be, gives you a hunch

Forgetting those small things,
The pain of doubt rings

Forgetting those small things,
Your heart seldom sings!

B. Easier Times

Easier times are what everyone longs for, those which preclude struggles, offering or promising joy and happiness. According to Goleman (1995), one of the main biological changes accompanying happiness is an increase in available energy, and a quieting of negative feelings that foster and generate worrisome thought. He points out, however, that there is no particular shift in physiology other than "a quiescence," facilitating the body's quicker recovery from "the biological arousal of upsetting emotions." The body is offered a "general rest," and there is more readiness and enthusiasm for whatever task presents itself, with more interest in a greater variety of goals.

In considering easier times, the two sections of poetry that follow focus on states that are known to promote lighter feelings. Whether they occur consecutively or independently, each opens the way for the realisation of the other. They are "Hope/Relief" and "Love."

1. Relief

Relief is what can lift us out of difficult feelings, excites our imagination, and fuels our desire to go on. Craib (1994) remarks, "One of the difficulties of living in our world is that it is perhaps increasingly less clear exactly what we might expect or hope for or desire." Then, taking this further, he states, "If the world won't match up to our ideals, then we must try to force it; if we ourselves don't match up to our ideals, then we punish and try to force ourselves."

The poems included here consider various ways of achieving states of hope and relief. Other people, objects, activities, and ourselves are all shown to contribute to elevations of mood, and even a young puppy at play can teach us a lot. Sometimes it is important to resolve to cherish what we have.

(1) Wanted

Wanted,
Needed again,
Relied on

Demanded,
Requested again,
Counted on

Feelings of pride,
Nothing to hide.

(2) Talking It Out

Talking it out,
Letting someone know

Talking it out,
Letting feelings show

By unveiling concerns and admitting fears,
There's comfort from others for your tears.

(3) The Light At The End Of The Tunnel

The light at the end of the tunnel,
A view through a long funnel

At times like these,
Nothing can please
At times like these,
Life seems to freeze

No solution to sit and sob,
Get out there, break self-defences,
Open the door, turn the knob

No one can help,
No one will help

Power over self,
The sole solution.

(4) Changed

Changed
Don't want to go back
Having gained,
Won't accept attack

A new sway,
A new day
More sensitive to feel, hear, see, touch, smell,
Really doing very well

The days have been long,
Emotions strong
After much discomfort and pain,
Sincerely aware of how much not to restrain

Now it's time to advance,
Keep this healthy stance

(5) Yes, There Are Some Nice People Around

Yes, there are some nice people around
Few and far between to be found,
But, there are some nice people around

And, how to reach them, the path isn't always straight,
Curves and bends may lead to a barred gate

And how to reach them, access isn't always clear,
However, once a lock's removed, you know you're near

With many closed doors, you may come face-to-face,
Then, when one opens for you, your heart starts to race

In life, we have to try every lock,
Knock after knock

In life, we have to keep on top,
Stop after stop

And, sometimes, we feel that we'll never arrive
But,
It's just at those times we must continue to strive

(6) Dessert

Carrot cake, cheese cake,
Fixation on dessert
Date square, pecan pie,
Strong need for heavy sigh

No meal complete,
Without some little treat

Calories at stake,
Pounds to intake

No special reason why

...Habit

Perfect excuse and ritual alibi.

(7) Not Eating Alone

At least you were not on your own,
Not another night of eating alone
And who knows where this hospitality might lead,
Another outing, maybe a return feed.

(8) Winning Smile

Smile beaming,
Radiance streaming
Messages from inside,
Emotions just won't hide

Something causing this high,
Curling those lips to the sky
Reasons behind the grinning,
Definite sense of winning.

(9) Happiness On My Mind

Happiness on my mind,
The day feels very kind

That I'm on a journey going somewhere,
At last I feel

That I've alleviated a heavier care,
My life may now be "real"

Reel with wonder and excitement
Heavy with new-found, long-awaited enlightenment

So, a new chapter, hopefully, begins.

(10) The Little Grape

It rolled across my kitchen floor
Immediate prey

Then out into the hallway

It followed us to the elevator
Then into the garage

A mesmerising force
Such a little grape

A mesmerising force
At least for a puppy at play

Oh, that my life be so simple.

(11) To Do Better

To cherish what I have
and realise its worth
To not complain
and be mindful of others' fates

To be able to be alone
and only accountable to myself

To stave off negative encounters
and know the abuse/rejection that they promote

To be aware of the forces outside of myself
and so permit the sands of time and possibility to shift
for the better

2. Love

This is a "highlight" of our easier times: (wo)man's ultimate comfort; to love and be loved. Goleman (1995) discusses the feelings that love engenders and what emanates from them.

Tender feelings, and sexual satisfaction entail parasympathetic arousal–the physiological opposite of the 'fight or flight ' mobilization shared by fear and anger. The parasympathetic pattern, dubbed the 'relaxation response,' is a bodywide set of reactions that generates a general state of calm and contentment, facilitating cooperation.

Most of the poems included here focus on the earlier stages of the love relationship, its enchantment and the positivity generated by it. The first and last poems, however, remind us that love may not always be available to all of us or easily maintained. The final poem about the unconditional love of a pet will strike a chord with many today. The ownership of a dog, cat, or some other cudddly creature is vital to the well-being of the many of us who live alone without possibility of an intimate human relationship.

(1) Love

I wanted to find love,
But where did it go?

Love escaped me: why?
I don't know

I wanted to find love,
But it never lasted for long

Love passed me by
Why?
I was never wrong!

(2) Feeling Great

Feeling great,
Whole week date

Days flow into days,
Learning each others' ways

Nights blissfully spent,
Some things are heaven sent.

(3) Sometimes Something Just Goes

Highs and lows,
Sometimes something just goes

Unbelievable but true
Yes, it can happen to you

Not only in movies and to friends
Your road too can take those bends

Bends of delight
Lots of happiness in sight

Warmth and smiles
Energy that will take you miles.

(4) Tender Moments

Head spinning
Heart fluttering
A lot of muttering

Clear calm eyes and
Smiling lips
Endless skies and
Idyllic trips
Warmth, tenderness and affection
A good feeling,
A healthy direction.

(5) Thinking of You

I was thinking of you
You were thinking of me

Neither of us knew
Each one was filled with glee

Activities and messages full of care
Wanting the other to be there

Doing and giving
A nice way of living

(6) To The New Person

Out of the blue
Came someone new

Passion, affection, consideration
An enticing new relation

Spontaneity, excitement, sincerity

Anxiousness to please
No games or tease

A better feeling every day
A new and wonderful way.

(7) The Couple

Sometimes it's only a matter of time
For the couple to find their rhyme

When adjustments can be made
Criticisms naturally fade
We live and learn
And sometimes burn

Man's quest for love, sometimes defying reason
It's often necessary for a relationship to travel through every season.

(8) Falling in Love

I spent Sunday
falling in love with my dog

Watching her
Touching her
Smelling her
Listening to her
Holding her

And she was there for me.

SECTION THREE: ACTIVITIES

Activities are what can take us away from, interrupt, or affect our relationships and feelings and vice versa; our distractions and interactions. According to Goleman (1995), "Actions that spring from the emotional mind carry a particularly strong sense of certainty, a by-product of a streamlined, simplified way of looking at things that can be absolutely bewildering to the rational mind." He refers to comments made by Ekman, that it is the fact that we cannot choose the emotions that we have that allows people to excuse their actions by saying that they were "in the grip of emotion."

The two sections of poetry that follow consider two main types of activities: those that are distracting, and those that are interactive. They are "Distractions" and "Interactions."

A. DISTRACTIONS

Distractions are our obligations, responsibilities and relaxation opportunities, that both give us routines and take us out of routines: work, studies, vacations, and pastimes. Goleman (1995) talks about the importance of distraction, particularly in attempting to interrupt depressing thoughts which have an automatic nature. Even if people try to suppress them, once the "depressive tide of thought" has started, they often cannot come up with better alternatives because of its "powerful magnetic effect on the train of association."

In considering distractions, the subsections that follow look at obligatory as well as optional activities. They are "Work," "Studies," "Vacations," and "Pastimes."

1. Work

Without work we cannot sustain our families and might not put our days, talents, interests or energies to their best use. Bly et al. (1993) believe that work is the first way of recognizing community. They also consider its relationship to love, "Work is often coupled with love as its opponent or substitute, as if each were an escape from the other."

The poems included here cover a number of phases of the work cycle: the hunt for work, its attainment and associated possibilities, maintenance, and the distractions that it serves.

(1) The Job-Hunt

Another day of attack,
But, what do you get back?

Aggress, assert,
But don't be hurt!

Boldness, strength,
Try the full day's length!

You're at that stage in between,
You long for someone/something to intervene!

Almost there, it's not a time to give in,
Tomorrow, who knows, a chance to win!

(2) New Work Prospects

A new idea, a new hope

A new distraction, a new rope

Challenge makes you shine,
Glory ultimately to be thine!

Encouraging opportunity to descend,
To deflation, putting an end

Impetus and drive,
You must imbue

Bringing this project alive,
The onus is on you!

(3) On Call For Work

Out of reach,
A juicy peach

Being there,
A weighty care

As a means of survival,
No other rival

When underemployed,
A massive void

Occupation,
Rationalisation

Work is key,
Commitment and liberty.

(4) A First Contract

Excitement builds, tension mounts,
Must win this contract on all counts!

Convincing and organized,
Inadequacies disguised

With bright ideas,
New fears
A chance to learn,
A chance to earn

This first job,
No one will rob
The first contract is a gateway,
No competition can take it away!

(5) Professional Ladders

Ladders are lowered in front of your face,
But, can you keep up the pace?

Ladders are lowered, going in all directions
But, can you climb up in sections?

The time has come to rise from the ground,
But, will your balance be sound?

The time has come to put perfection aside,
Fussiness inhibits a wider stride

Professional ladders, opportunities that are open to all

Climb them for what they are

Don't even think about the fall!

(6) Professional Success

Professional success,
But what about a personal life?

Professional success,
But what about a husband or wife?

Professional success,
Is it really a solution?

Professional success,
There's not always appropriate retribution.

(7) Staying On My Journey

My journey went well today,
I didn't look back
No self-recrimination or attack

"Hooray" for professional success!
Not to regress!

I have to remind myself to persevere,
That danger is always near

No matter how well I do
The emotions' forces always brew

Why can't I stay on track?
Concentrate on my own journey?

When work goes well, I should have it all
Why should others' intimate misbehaviour be my downfall?

My heart swells

The pain is raw
I need more

Oh, to be strong!

(8) Another Day of Killing Time

On with the task
Another day of killing time

On with the task
But you don't forget your sorrows

On with the task
There but not there, functioning for others

On with the task
Another day of killing time.

(9) Throwing Myself Into My Work

Work, work, work
Distract, distract, distract

Focus, focus, focus
Produce, produce, produce

Then, when the task is done
A new day will begin

Or, so they say

Then, when the task is done
You'll be a stronger person

Or, so they say

Then, when the task is done
You'll be in the same "stuck place"

That's what I say!

2. Studies

With more knowledge we may be presented with the opportunity to go further at work, at play, and in our personal lives. Howard Gardner (1993) states, "Through formal tutoring, or through literature, rituals, and other symbolic forms, the culture helps the growing individual to make discriminations about his own feelings or about the other persons in his milieu." However, as Goleman (1995) points out, "Academic intelligence offers virtually no preparation for the turmoil —or opportunity—life's vicissitudes bring."

The poems included here focus both on positive and negative aspects of being absorbed in studies, from the curative properties of distraction to the stresses and strains of managing too much or poorly presented knowledge. The final two poems indicate possible challenges as studies reach completion.

(1) Emotional Overload

Emotional overload,
You think you're going to explode

Intellectual learning,
In your cranium
Has every cell burning

So much capacity,
So little elasticity

You never expected such dimension,
A challenge to your memory,
Its retention

You never expected so much stimulation,
Of so many new questions, the generation.

(2) Studying As Cure

Head ache
Face ache
Back ache
Bone ache

The end of a long year

Another day to study...

Just the cure,
A time to fight your war!

Time to succeed,
Simple instructions: look, listen, read

When studying does the job,
No time to sob

Then, when the day is over...

You've walked the rope,
Blotted out problems and tried to cope

Feeling lousy,
Even drowsy

...But progress has been made.

(3) Presence At A Workshop

Being at a workshop
But not being there

To distraction, you always hop,
And, at the point of being absorbed, lose all sense of care

Not here,
Not there,
Not anywhere!

Killing time and feeling ill at ease,
Putting yourself through a workshop is only a tease!

(4) The Mature Student

Back at school,
Wasted time to unspool
Boring presentations,
Inconsequential revelations

Five months more,
Time I abhor

And then,
The end

A totally new bend

A chance to follow my own rules,
Use new tools

Perseverance required,
An imagination that's fired

(5) Graduation

Graduation,
No Elation

Even after graduation,
Of your personal problems,
There's no cessation...

Graduation,
What for?

Nothing can reopen a closed door!

(6) School's Over

Trains, planes, boats, cars,
I gaze at the stars

Journeys near, journeys far,
I'd like to be where you are
The grass is greener on the other side,
It's not a time to hide

It's time to move on from here
However, the next destination is not near

Struggles, confusion, doubt
Often I feel the need to shout

Impatient to be there,
I stop and stare

The end is almost in sight
Everything feels right

3. Vacation

Sometimes we need a break from routine (work, studies, or personal situations) to recharge and refresh our energies. Miranda Seymour (1996), in her biography of the poet Robert Graves, talks about the important impact school vacations made on him. This lasted throughout his life, being a strong influence on his writings. She states, "Although Graves went to his first three schools in Wimbledon, London made little impact on him. His strongest memories of childhood were associated with Germany and North Wales where he spent his school holidays." Seymour elaborates, "Bavaria gave him a rich cluster of childhood memories and a working knowledge of German; the mountains and moors of North Wales gave him an enduring source of myth and imagery."

The poems included here focus on the exhilarating effects of vacations, the new energy that is found at those times, and different reasons for its generation.

(1) Joyful Anonymous Traveller

Regaling and sailing

Excited and delighted

Cares lifting,
Mind drifting

Adventures and explorations
Awakening new sensations

Incognito to revel,
Mysteries to unravel

Joyful anonymous traveller!

(2) Vacation Over

Relaxed

Unwound

Vacation well-passed,
Happy thoughts and memories abound

Satisfied,
Rested,
Contented
Tranquillity found

(3) Vacation High

Organized,
A high of feeling on top

Motivated,
No time to stop

Relaxed,
Dissatisfaction and discontent no longer lurk

Refreshed,
Total readiness and enthusiasm for work

When in that spin,
All can win!

4. Pastimes

On a daily basis or when we cannot take a vacation, it is good to be able to choose to have something different to focus our energies on, particularly if it is creative. Moore (1996) talks about the many people he meets "who are able to avoid falling into easy modern despair" despite having suffered great hardships. They "cultivate their love of life in gardening, painting, travel, music, and community service."

The first poem included here emphasizes consequences of not allowing for free time. The others consider various activities and objects involved in the pursuit of pastimes.

(1) Postponed Pleasure

You postponed your pleasure,
So where's the treasure?

You postponed your pleasure,
So where's your leisure?

An investment in your future you made,
When, in the present you should have played

Mistake!

(2) The Writing Circle

A cramped little room,
Faces eager in anticipation

A confined vacuum,
Participants anxious for relation,
Creative sensation

Bland setting: low ceiling, vacant walls
And, through the window, another leaf falls

Fall beckons; its sunlight and fresh air
Fall, through the open window, I'd rather be there

Cars in the driveway, life outside
Today's a day to deny that pleasure,
Stay on the inside

Inside today, some seeds will be planted,
Nothing that's said taken for granted

How to play with words will be taught,
Then...
With the writing bug you'll be caught.

(3) Writing On Demand

Writing on demand,
Emotions made bland

Forced inspiration
Numbed sensation
Poetry through discipline,
A notion that's wearing thin

When the pen doesn't flow,
Thoughts just won't grow.

(4) Eagerness To Paint

Art inspires,
Art fires
Paint flows

Desire and burn,
Eagerness to learn

Enthusiasm radiates

Haste not possible,
Perfection responsible

Productivity in moderation,
Deliberation and concentration

Art, so much painstaking care,
Art, such expression to share

(5) Using Art As Therapy

Confused and fragmented,
Overwhelmed and distracted

Lucid moments meet obstacles,
Barriers create hurdles

Larger than life or disengaged,
Lost in an abyss, my life is staged

A cacophony and crisis, holes and gaps,
No road maps

Energy dispelled through interaction,
Spaces and colour providing much attraction

Action happens within a boundary, the need for containment,
Creativity providing chaos and excitement.

(6) The Baker

Full of heavy care,
She bakes into the night
How long can she this stormy weather fare?
Keep up the fight?

'Phone a friend, she thinks,
But, to what end?
Every response stinks

"Call me another day!"
"I'm busy with my mother, father, husband, child!"
"No time to listen to anything wild!"

She's on her own

Another day goes by,
How long before someone will hear her cry?

(7) Ode On Natchos

Piquant sensation,
Cheesy revelation

Sour cream drips,
A licking of lips

Salt addicts,
Inner conflicts
Diet out of sight,
Avocado rich but light
Desire for more,
Cucumber, pepper, tomato draw
Mountain diminishing,
Everything finishing

Appetite satisfied,
Craving pacified

And, on the 'morrow, a savouring,
A need to work out, punitive labouring.

(8) A First Workout

Poor abdominal...

One evening of exercise,
Hardly a surprise

Consistency's the key,
Fosters the ache-free

...The ingredients for feeling good,
A body that works the way that it should!

(9) Tarot

Can you really change your pattern and fate?

Is there really an open gate?

How did I do it?
How will I maintain it?

A good sensation is what I'm feeling,
My tarot card reading was so revealing!

(10) Headline News: The Death of a Princess

A princess died today
Died,
Like anyone else

A princess died today
But,
Not like anyone else

With glory
Comes attention,
Good and bad

With glory
Comes mention,
Wanted or not

The world is stunned,
Shocked...

But what about
The man in the street
Who lost his wife

To cancer
AIDS
Assault

A car crash
That shakes the world,
Puts life in perspective

Is louder
Than the loss of the man in the street

Sometimes it takes
An icon
To wake up the world

To appreciate
What was
And,
Could have been

To rethink how
We all behave

The impact of
One life on the world
On others' stories...

That have not been
told or
heard

B. Interactions

Interactions are what transpire between individuals, others, and the world, explaining, redirecting, or interrupting our course. Goleman

(1995) describes how "Gardner noted that the core of interpersonal intelligence includes the 'capacities to discern and respond appropriately to the moods, temperaments, motivations, and desires of other people.'" Nowinski (1993) points out the differences between men's and women's ways of relating, stating, "Sadly, many men experience a woman's desire to communicate in the same way that she would with other women as something threatening and terrifying."

In considering interactions, the subsections that follow look at self, other, and circumstances, in situations that may necessitate confrontation, or direction for appropriate outcomes to ensue. They are "Challenges" and "Communications."

1. Challenges

Sometimes our routines and habits come up against ways or obstacles that are not easy or sure. Rutter and Rutter (1993) discuss how "we are all thinking, feeling beings and our thought processes in terms of self-images, self-concepts, internal working models and attributional styles will influence how we deal with life transitions and challenges." They also describe the influences on these "thought processes": they are either "self-perpetuating (through habit and practice)," or, "open to change (through the effects of new and different experiences)." Therefore, different situations will arouse different responses in different people.

The poems included here describe mood states and their mental, physical, and societal blocks and stimulants. They also consider circumstances that are beyond individual or human control, and possible obstacles encountered when undergoing transitions. It is not always external forces that interrupt our progress. We can sometimes be our own hindrances when we do not take risks.

(1) Dear Anger

Dear Anger,

You grow day by day,
For brief moments only, you go away

Not to have you there, I don't know how that would be,
You're not the nicer side of me!

Not to have you there, I want that to be,
But where will be my authenticity?
It's taken so long for you to come out,
To release that shout
And now I'm there, we're there,
You're such a heavy care!

Please tell me what you're trying to say to me?
That I'm getting there day by day,
That we've come a long way,
That you're here for a while to stay,
That you're keeping me on the right way!

I thank you for being there,
Dear Anger!

(2) Phobic

Total rigidity

The mind won't work,
The body wants to shirk

Fear to come, fear to go,
Afraid to say "yes," afraid to say "no"

Looking for excuses,
Ready to be tied up in nooses!

Easy to give in,
Lose all sense of discipline

Hard to break out,
To find the voice to shout.

(3) Following The Rules

Yes, the rules

No, the rules
Of course, the rules

I've followed them all along
But, did they make me better?
Or, did they make me strong?
Wrong, wrong, wrong!

Those who stick to the rules,
They treat themselves as fools

Others who are more smart,
Give themselves a head start

Without rules,
Life unspools

With more possibilities,
There's less internal hostilities

With more openness to chance,
Comes weakened compliance

Rules are meant to be broken,
A reminder that is too seldom spoken!

(4) Pull Yourself Together!

With confusion and doubt,
Disorganization comes about

Pull yourself together!

Your weeks of preparation,
Hours of dedication

All can be undone in a day

It's easy to give in

A constant battle to stay on top,
Not to stop!

Don't question,
Encourage action
Self-indulgence is not recommended,
Self-pity cannot be defended

Time wasted never returns,
Involvement's the only way one learns

The more you do, the more you will,
Limitations, capacities, opportunities finally recognized
Through coming to terms, happiness may be realized

(5) Realization Of Limitation

Realization of limitation

Hesitation,
Rejection,
Contemplation

Towards hope, no inclination

(6) Stuck in the Same Place

Ever look around
And everyone in your circle has moved on

Ever look around
And no one's left to carry on

What happened?
How did you get stuck?

What happened?
Who influenced your luck?
A quirk of fate,
Something you could not instigate

(7) Synchronicity (in 2 parts)

Part one: The Truth

To know the truth,
Would that be better
To know the truth,
Could you handle the pain?

In knowing the truth,
There'd be an end to the imagination's game

Part two: Coincidences

Coincidences,
They happen for a reason

Coincidences,
They uncover treason

Right place, right time
Wrong person

Right place, right time,
You yourself see the true version

Having actually seen them with your own eyes,
You know his real interest with another lies

Now, finally,
Accept that his explanations are no more than alibis!

(8) From Creation to Fruition

Creation
Elation

Then...
Irritation,
Procrastination,
Annihilation

Will it work ?
Is it right?
Are your dreams out of sight?
Doubts and fears
The day of realisation nears

A deep breath, a heavy sigh
Now's not a good time to cry!

Then it's done -- fruition!
Finally recognition

Alas!...
But that's only the start!
A time to leap

Brace the heart.

(9) From Fantasy to Reality

Fantasies about what could be,
You and me

Fantasies about what should be,
You and me

But, moving from the fantasy to reality,
A hard step to take

Moving from the fantasy to reality,
Nothing can be fake

For that moment, you long
And, in the meantime, no option,
Other than to be strong

(10) After A Car Accident

Lost, confused,
What to do?

Alone, abused
Who to talk to?

Independence versus support,
Pride versus shame

Expecting retort
How long to play the game?

Absurd rules,
Problems, inconvenience, hastles

Then, when the heat cools,
Visits to those bureaucratic castles!

Denying the temptation to complain,
Holding it in

Patience without gain
No chance to win!

(11) Don't Bother Me, I've Just Been Born

Don't bother me
I know where I'm going

I've just,
Yes, I've just

Been born
Finally, I 've grown up

Don't bother me
I'm doing the work

I've just
Definitely just

Been born
I have learned from experience

Don't bother me
I need to be left alone
To get there sooner

I've just,
More than just,
Totally finished

Being born
I'm ready to activate
Regenerate

Live a new self

(12) Taking The Risk

Stuck is familiar
              painful
                 unending

Stuck is inflexible
                 inescapable
                 self-defeating

Breaking free takes courage

Breaking free takes time

Breaking free takes risk

And, on the outside of the hole
Predictability is gone

And, on the outside of the hole
Relief is uncertain

But, on the inside of the hole
the life force is gone

So,
What's the risk?

To try another way
possibly

2. Communications

Certain challenges come our way that involve communications issues whilst other communications can be "interesting" in and of themselves. Caroline Knapp (1994) asks, "What happens to the other feelings that leap into your heart when you act so grown-up and mature? What happens to the part of you that wants to scream and pout? And what happens to the suspicion lurking deep in your soul that a lot of the behaviors you're asked to be mature about are often rude and selfish?"

The poems included here consider individual identities and needs as well as connections that might be made with others: our interactions are often affected by our perceptions of others' dispositions. The final poem, which focuses on a need for non-verbal communication, reminds us (ironically) that words are not for everyone.

(1) Who Am I?

Sometimes shy,
Sometimes sly

Often sad,
Often glad

At times internally mad.

(2) All I Want To Do Is Talk

Silence
Cold, dark, blank silence

All I want to do is talk

That's all I've ever wanted, needed, pleaded,

Tongue in cheek whispers and glances,
You remain totally preoccupied with your own advances

Yes, you think that you know better,
Boasting of your own latest caper

And you wonder why the "good little girl" is able to disappear,
Well, she no longer knows why she is here.

(3) Talking Too Much

Talking too much,
Revealing too much

Chance for a friend,
Permission to let introspection end

Temptation of giving out all,
Forever in combat for withdrawal

Different personalities,
Changing realities

Staying on guard,
Really hard

Talking too much,
Losing too much

(4) Communication Games

That knowing glance,
That glint in the eye

A changing in stance,
Or hint of the shy

The games people play,
More unintelligible every day

The communications that they make,
Hard to distinguish true from fake
Then, when the time comes for the facade to be lifted,
Real discoveries are made,
Feelings shifted.

(5) Eye On Someone

Eye on someone,
Letting them know

Liking someone,
But not having it show
A delicate game to play,
The experienced, however, have proven a way

When time is short,
How to have the right glance caught

No hard and fast rule
But,
The projection of nonchalance seems to fool!

(6) In Authority

Recognized, respected,
Considered worthwhile
Praised and comprehended,
Sure of a smile

To this position of authority,
You were singled out from the majority

The merit you may have earned,
But, from experience you should have learned

There are no real moments of glory,
Other people will adjust your story.

(7) Her Struggle: Hold Your Tongue

As you watch her struggle, you interject
Her response: reject, reject, reject!

No advice will she take,
Her opinion's better what ever the stake!

As you watch her body give in,
You know that she can't win

Hold your tongue, keep your thoughts in
Her issues not being yours,
Your own life must begin!

(8) To Be Handled With Kid Gloves

Lest what you say should offend,
You keep your tongue guarded; bend, bend, bend

Does the other realise how hard you try,
Their frailty not to deny?

(9) I Had a Bad Day Too

You've had enough,
That's tough

A life of ease,
Please don't tease

I had a bad day too,
Don't want to know about you!

(10) Communicating Feelings: Does He Really Care?

From letting myself get carried away,
I stray

About letting myself get carried away,
What's getting in the way?
I want him to feel and be there,
But does he really care?

I want him only, resigned to his short-comings,
But, what's behind his hummings?
Please may he be ready, I pray,
Remove all the obstacles from his way

Only let me get carried away
Knowing that with me, he'll stay.

(11) Revelation

So many words, too many words

A muzzinness descends
Beyond words

On the path there have been
Only words

And,
Words alone
Don't work for me

Art,
I need art

I need actual pictures
As well as words
To reach my heart

Images in poetic language
That merely describe
Resonate
But don't quite elevate

A concrete visual
Image
Speaking louder than words
Complements those words

Words without
Art
Drift from my heart

SECTION FOUR: NATURAL FORCES

Natural forces are what is there or happens despite ourselves (our relationships, feelings, and activities) and tends to involve the environment and the body. For instance, Bly et al. (1993) talk about how "Moments come when we feel outside time, seized by a longing, moved by an image, in touch with invisible voices."

The two sections of poetry that follow consider two specific entities affected by natural forces, "The Environment" and "The Body."

A. The Environment

Locations, climates and time regulators outside of the body can change and be changed in ways that are usually out of our control. Rutter and Rutter (1993) comment, "Most discussions of environmental influences on development tend to assume that they have much the same effect on everyone. Yet it is obvious with ordinary life circumstances that individuals vary greatly in how they respond to the same stress stimulus." Considering this further, Molly Harrower (1995) affirms that the relationship between mood and environmental characteristics or atmosphere is not a simple one. "One and the same physical environment can call out different feelings in the same person at different times, to say nothing of different feelings in two people at the same time."

In considering the environment, the subsections that follow look at both natural and man-made components. They are "Nature," "Weather," and "The Calendar."

165

1. *Nature*

Elements in the settings around us can have lives of their own beyond human existence, that may cause us to wonder or be impediments to our well-being. Considering the extremes, Rutter and Rutter (1993) discuss the role of chance, particularly in the occurrence of "the major natural and man-made disasters such as earthquakes, volcanoes, floods, plane crashes and shipwrecks." Kay Redfield Jamison (1994) discusses how extremes and contrasts in the natural world are among the most commonly used metaphors in art.

The first two poems included here consider aspects of nature's power and physical features. The last three focus on time, a tangible and measurable force in western context, and an intransigent entity in eastern thought. In poem number six, the little bird serves as "fly on the wall."

(1) *Nature*

Nature, dear loyal friend,
Ever present to seek,
No end

Nature's loyalty,
Overwhelming,
Her supremacy, a reality

Majestic in her regulation,
A power without condition.

(2) *Sea, Sand, Sun*

Sea and sand,
A freshness in the air

Sun on the face,
A warm embrace, kissing care

Nature's open arms,
Multiple charms

Healer, repairer, restorer,
Reviver and giver

Captivating and curing,
Very reassuring

Sea, sand sun,
A feeling of being at one.

(3) Time

Time,
The course of time

Time,
I'm relying on time

Time will do the work,
Time will let me shirk.

(4) Timing

To reach goals,
Always strings and controls

Timing, timing

...What keeps life rhyming.

(5) Time Moves On

The passage of time can be very fast,
Some days just whiz past

The passage of time is not in our control,
Our lives blinking by, without any chance of feeling whole.

(6) Little Bird

Little bird in the tree
You know what's going on

Camouflaged and disguised
You take it all in
What's happening all around

Those branches that bud and bloom
The ones that go on to produce seeds
Make new trees grow

And those that are left barren
Still have a place on the tree
But not continuity

Little bird,
observer of her environment's destiny

Beyond, at the blue sky
You look

Another environment to fly on to,
To overlook.

2. Weather

Climactic constancies and extremes have effects on our daily lives and feeling states. Bly et al. (1993) also describe human behaviour as being vulnerable to similar transitions and inclemencies. They state, "Of course any earthly loving is subject to seasons, sudden storms, and droughts. And whoever can tie together can tear asunder."

The first three poems included here focus on types of weather, and reactions to it, in particular those prominent in the Canadian climate. The final poem uses weather as metaphor, "Sorrow like ceaseless rain..."

(1) First Snow

Snow,
Please go!

Snow,
Oh no!
Attractive to the eye,
Disastrous for moving by

Powdery and white,
A pretty sight

Slushy and grey,
A hazard in the way

Cold, wet, slimy,
Restricting, confining, grimy
In the mountains, beautiful, a pleasure,
Great for lovers of winter leisure

In the city, a danger, an awe,
Makes mobility a hazardous chore

Snowfall not abating,
Entrapment imposed that's irritating

Salted, shovelled, defeated,
Man as victor
Snow's unseated!

(2) Rain on Sunday

Rain, rain go away,
Come again another day

Sunday's a "fun day,"
Should be a Monday

On Monday there's room,
For a little more gloom

Sunday should be bright,
A day filled with light.

(3) Sun

Sun,
A real treasure to be won

Wonderful, wonderful sun
Exhilarating,
Revitalizing

Warm, caressing sun,
Days without you,
Are days undone

Energy and light,
All feels right
Sun's deity, brightness, gaiety

Sun,
Awakener of positive sensations
Wonderful, wonderful sun.

(4) Renaissance / The Cycle of Life

Sorrow like ceaseless rain
But the rain does stop

Sorrow like ceaseless rain
but floods do come to an end

After hurricanes, tropical storms
Towns rebuild

After brush fires
The forest renews

A fresh chance
A new start

A moment to be
In the order of nature

Nature all knowing
Destiny all showing

Without sadness
No real joy

Without loss
Nothing to excite and fill a space

Sorrow, like ceaseless rain
Facilitator
Of joy,
A life to duly regain.

3. The Calendar

The calendar organizes our days by giving us times of year and schedules: sometimes time works for us, and at others, against us; occasionally we are "in sync." Jamison (1994) describes how the rotations of the earth around the sun, and of the moon around the earth serve to regulate life on cellular, biochemical, physiological, and psychological levels. Roland (1988) is particularly interested in the difference between eastern and western relationships with time. "The West has developed linear, historical theories of social events; in Hindu culture time is essentially ahistorical and mythological: in recurrent cycles through festivals, holidays, rituals, and such there is repetition and reintegration into life of the mythological and divine presence."

The poems included here consider specific junctures in the western calendar and incumbent routines, aspirations, and mind-sets. It is, therefore, interesting to consider here, any relationship to Jamison's (1994) research findings concerning poets', novelists', and visual artists' pronounced seasonal patterns: poets and novelists report that their greatest artistic productivity occurs during September, October, and November.

(1) A New Year's Starting

Everything's going to be fine

A new year's starting,
Old trepidations parting

A new leaf to turn,
Old doubts to burn
Start positive!

(2) February and November

February and November,
Gloomy as burnt ember

End of Autumn
End of Winter

Pre-Christmas
Pre-Spring

Time for doubt,
A need to shout

Long cycles filled with lows,
Stress seldom goes

February and November,
Times not to remember.

(3) Autumn Approaches

Season of misty and mellow fruitfulness,
The time of the Jewish new year
Days to confess, days to share

Change of season
Changes of heart
An opportunity for reason
Hope for a fresh start

Season of misty and mellow fruitfulness,
The time for going back to school
Days of freshness, days to be cool.

(4) The New School Year

The new school year has changed me,
Rekindled passion for self-directed learning rearranged me

When school is on my mind,
Leisure-time becomes more confined

With a somewhat eased heart,
I'm ready for a fresh academic start

Open to reaching new intellectual heights,
I steady myself for distracting flights

My personal self can disappear safely into the background.

B. The Body

The body and what happens to it in the course of our development and growth can be either beyond or in our control. However, we don't always have a choice. Jamison (1994) notes that although biological rhythms cycle synchronistically with celestial rhythms, they are clearly regulated by endogenous processes.

Coincidental to prominent themes in this book, Camille Paglia (1995) sees poetry as the connecting link between body and mind: "Every idea in poetry is grounded in emotion. Every word is a palpitation of the body. The multiplicity of interpretation surrounding a poem mirrors the stormy uncontrollability of emotion, where nature works her will. Emotion is chaos. Every benign emotion has a flip side of negativity."

In considering the body, the subsections that follow are concerned with natural processes, that may or may not be sequential and are often affected by individual, societal, or fatalistic interventions. They are "Health," "Illness," and "Aging."

1. Health

When we take care of our health or it takes care of us, other things tend to go more easily. Goleman (1995) notes how relationships may affect our health. "Negative relationships take their toll. The more significant the relationship is in your life, the more it matters for your health."

The poems included here indicate what might threaten the maintenance of good health as well as showing how individuals' health conditions may put them at a disadvantage no matter what happens. All may not be as is seen. Similarly, the hard work that goes into the acquisition of good health may be taken for granted.

(1) Sense Of Humour

Sense of humour,
Form of sanity

Moving along with the crowd,
Possibilities to let go and giggle out loud

So, what stops you, blocks you?
Why such contentment with shades of blue?

Ambiance to share,
Alleviator of massive care

Sense of humour,
Friend of humanity.

(2) Little Pill

Little pill,
Do what you will

Little pill,
You keep my health still

Now you're working,
My mind is eased

Now you're working,
My body's no longer teased

With iron reserves restored,
Vital functionings are no longer ignored
More productivity from energy levels rising

Tiny little pill,
You're quite surprising!

(3) Physically "In Condition"

A "fine form" that's bold and strong
Though, much is wrong

Physically "in condition"

Hidden,
Menacing mental attrition.

(4) Ode On Date Squares

Date with dates,
That sugary sensation that one loves but hates

Good friend,
Cravings just don't end
All too available in times of need,
To those multiple calories you easily concede

Feelings of greed,
Outer biscuit eaten with speed
Pangs of guilt,
Appetite starts to wilt

Momentary happiness,
...Problems are no less

(5) The Time of the Month

The time of the month again,
Too soon!

The time of the month again,
Another new moon!

Two good weeks out of every four,
What ripe woman can guarantee more?

(6) In the Age of AIDS

In the age of AIDS
Be smart!

Don't get carried away with your whole heart

Question!
Inform!
Research!

Be aware of all dangers,
You really don't know the past of handsome strangers!

(7) You With Your Baby

With your baby you looked so calm
Still extended your arm

In your own world, but still in others' too
This birth has only made a healthier you

The waiting, the readiness, and then his arrival
The challenges that you've overcome along the way

True survival

(8) The Pecan Assignment

Being given food
Puts me on my guard
Will we have to eat it?
Maybe it's something I'm allergic to...

Calm down
It's just going to be an exercise
But what if I'm not going to be able to experience
the whole exercise

Just as I don't seem to be experiencing
Other aspects of a whole life now

A small part of this pecan
just broke off
I hardly touched it
How fragile it can be?...
Just like me

A sliver detached
from the rest of the group
And the group goes on

Now, we have been told to eat the pecan
Correct!
I'm too nervous to try, worried about my consequences

Poor innocent pecan,
I crave to taste you like the others can
Maybe they can tell me how their experience was
Alas, our experiences cannot be the same, even as a group.

2. Illness

When we are impeded by ill health (physical and mental), struggles and incumbent learning experiences often emerge. Goleman (1995) says that Francisco Varela describes the immune system as the body's brain.

> Immune cells travel in the bloodstream throughout the entire body, contacting virtually every other cell. Those cells they recognize, they leave alone; those they fail to recognize they attack. The attack either defends us against viruses, bacteria, and cancer or, if the immune cells misidentify some of the body's own cells, creates an autoimmune disease such as allergy or lupus.

Goleman also refers to a study explaining how "people who experienced chronic anxiety, long periods of sadness and pessimism, unremitting tension or incessant hostility, relentless cynicism or suspiciousness, were found to have *double* the risk of disease—including asthma, arthritis, headaches, peptic ulcers, and heart disease."

The poems included here not only consider the state of being ill, but also reactions to illness, both of the sufferer and of those in the sufferer's life. Sometimes we behave in ways that disturb and upset us, familiar activities, aptitudes and character traits escaping our control.

(1) Another Flu

Utter frustration,
Complete incapacitation

Draining hopelessness,
Unmerciful illness

Life gets busy,
You get dizzy

Another flu,
And, about it, nothing you can do

Routines broken

(2) I'm Sick, Leave Me!

I'm sick,
We can forget it!

I'm sick

Don't see me or be with me
Yes, get on with your life!

I'm sick

Don't invest in me or console me
No, I'm not good material for wife !

I'm sick,
Leave me and forget it!

(3) Illness Taken Seriously

Illness denied,
You get really low
Illness accepted,
Your life's still ago

When should pains be taken seriously?
Sometimes they come and go quite mysteriously

When you're going down, it's hard to see
But, when you've arrived, it can be agony

The going back up can be very tough,
Energy levels never being enough

Every day challenging

Diet monitored
Lifestyle adjusted

Faith and hope entrusted

(4) STARTING TO "PIG"

Eating too much,
Starting to "pig"

Flabby to touch,
Growing big

A little willpower, self-restraint,
Exert it!
Don't give yourself cause for complaint

Easier to gain,
Harder to lose

Easy to attain,
Hard to refuse
Eating for comfort can't be allowed

Attack the problem at heart,
At least, make a start

Banish self-pity
Appearances to keep,
Benefits to reap

But, only if you're strong, attractive to bring along

Be sane,
It's to your gain

Eliminate compulsion.

(5) Frightened Underwear

I put my underwear on
sideways
And didn't know it

I did not know much

I put my underwear on sideways
And went about my day

I felt out of touch

A simple task
Became a major chore

What used to take a little
Took a whole lot more

I put my underwear on
Sideways

No one else knew it,
But I did

My deteriorating mind
Infuriated me
The me that used to be ME

The me I'm getting to know
Doesn't put on a good show

To herself there's no mask

What will appear next?
She's frightened to ask.

3. Aging

This is a process that we have limited control over that is often accompanied by ill health: in the '90s the trend is to fight it off whole-heartedly. Rutter and Rutter (1993) state:

At all ages people's psychological functioning tends to be most strongly influ-enced by factors operating at that time—be they maturational, genetic or envi-ronmental. However, the point that comes over repeatedly in longitudinal studies is that the outcome of transitions, and the ways in which they are dealt with, is partially determined by people's past behaviour and experiences.

The poems included here show sign posts appearing on journeys through life. Whether by old photographs, or a lost tooth, our person-al aging processes are responded to and marked.

(1) Age Creeps On

Age creeps on,
"Womens' complaints" appear

Time moves on,
Questions of fertility invoke fear

If you were married
Would you be so harried?

Because you remain alone,
Do you have justification to moan?
More justification, you say

Life, on other levels too,
Has just not gone your way!

(2) Old Photographs

Old photographs,
Not always a barrel of laughs

Tales of happier days,
Different ways
Your life was easier then,
And, compared to now, an Eden

What your life is today,
You can't compare in any way

You never realised your choices and chances,
Turned away stability and happy romances

At that time, what was in your head?

That you'd never get those options again,
No one ever said!

(3) Another Friend Engaged

Another friend engaged,

And you?

Still available,

The years go by...

With little hope left,
You cry
And cry
And cry...

But, on the inside of course,
No one should know your real pain

Never able to publicly complain!
So, what's your reward?

NOTHING!...NO ONE!

There's no compensation

Just because you didn't "settle"
That doesn't mean you're made of metal

Alone and aging,
It's hard to get satisfaction from career success

Alone and aging,
It's hard to put aside your emptiness

(4) Generation Gaps

Generation gaps,
Laps and laps and laps!

Getting bigger by the day,
Especially when they want to have their way

Generation gaps,
Laps and laps and laps!

Getting bigger in every way,
Especially when they don't listen to what you have to say.

(5) A Cracked Tooth

What happened to my tooth,
My youth?

I took you for granted

Then,
In one innocent bite,

A motion in time
You were cracked,
Broken, defeated,
Gone
No longer a living part of me

For more than thirty years you'd been there
Unconditionally
But, with every bite I took,
My concentration was always somewhere else
On the food, conversation, time,
But not on you

You who facilitated my activity,
Helped my silently,
Lovingly,
Knowingly
I took foregranted
Thought could be repaired,
Ground down, filled, capped,
Preserved in my mouth
But, alas,
Infection was spreading around

So, I felt you for a last time
Sucked you,
Licked you,
Kissed you goodbye
While you were still a part of me

Before that final yank.

PART THREE

SCAPING WITH YOUR OWN WORDS

Some of the greatest lines of poetry have been and are written or spoken by people of minimum or no formal education.
                                                                Arthur Lerner, 1982

Chapter I

WORDSCAPING 101

When writing poetry "for product" there are grammatical rules and stylistic restrictions to keep in mind. However, when writing poetry "for therapy" they can all be put aside. Whatever words spring to mind and in whichever way they might be arranged on the page is generally acceptable. If, per chance, there is some order (conventional or otherwise) to the lines' composition and placement, it is an added bonus. Schloss and Grundy (1994) discuss their experience with poems written for therapy:

> A client may or may not produce a work that is esthetically appealing and worth considering by others as having artistic value. The therapist, however, is not primarily concerned with the aesthetics of the poem. For him, the work is a vehicle for helping the client explore himself. This exploration, not the poem itself, is paramount. The poem, then, expresses the heightened emotions of the client, whether it reflects artistic merit or not.

The exercises offered here provide the opportunity for unconscious thoughts and feelings to come to the surface, be identified, and where is necessary or possible, be explored further. The majority of exercises involve list-making or short descriptive tasks that are designed to trigger series of free rather than guided associations. As Daniel Goleman (1995) stated in his book, *Emotional Intelligence*: "The logic of the emotional mind is associative; it takes elements that symbolize a reality, or trigger a memory of it, to be the same as that reality. That is why similes, metaphors, and images speak directly to the emotional mind, as do the arts–novels, film, poetry, song, theatre, opera."

189

Also, when creating lists or following association-related sequences, there is usually more spontaneity and pictorial language. Focusing on or prioritizing sentence constructions can detract from the freshness of a piece, making it too deliberate, and lacking in the surprises that unexpected imagery of the moment can offer. Self-discovery through poetry and otherwise, is usually more authentic without preplanning structures, intentional theme division, or overdirection from others.

Arthur Lerner (1994) refers to Anne Stanford in discussing how poetry can be described as "the language of analogies." Connections in poetry being associational as well as causal; patterns that come forth in finished form in the structure of the poem are constructed by the psyche. Consequently, the relationships seen among objects by poets are usually significant for everyone.

On a different but related note, Kay Redfield Jamison (1994) considered J.P. Guilford's series of systematic psychological studies into the nature of creativity. His definitions attached to "fluency of thinking," "spontaneous flexibility," and "adaptive flexibility" are of particular interest here, in the context of the selection of exercises that follow. "Fluency of thinking," Guilford defined as being measured by specific tasks:

> Word fluency, the letter or combination of letters; associational fluency, the production of as many synonyms as possible for a given word in a limited amount of time; expressional fluency, the production and rapid juxtaposition of phrases or sentences; and ideational fluency, the ability to produce ideas to fulfil certain requirements in a limited amount of time.

Guilford described "spontaneous flexibility," as "The ability and disposition to produce a great variety of ideas, with freedom to switch from category to category," and "adaptive flexibility" as "The ability to come up with unusual types of solutions to set problems" (Jamison, 1994).

Jamison (1994), herself, points out how making connections between opposites which is crucial to the creative process is also important generally for the seeing of resemblances between previously unassociated conditions or objects. Jamison's (1994) particular interest, however, is in manic depressive illness, being both a sufferer from it herself, and eminent researcher in the field. The ability to rhyme, pun, and make sound associations is seen to increase with the energy surge that mania entails. Noting how manic individuals will often start writing poetry spontaneously, she cites research studies that record how word associational capabilities are increased as many as three times.

The research volunteers who contributed the poems in the examples that follow, included with each exercise, taught me a lot. No matter how clear directives are for expressive exercises, there will still be more interpretations of them than the person who prepared them could ever imagine. Therefore, even though there are a couple of options included for some of the tasks. I am sure that the reader/wordscapes will find many more possibilities for originality.

An important aspect of the exercises to keep in mind is that the finished poems should be named. Giving a poem a name can give the words a feeling of focus, and the person who has brought them together a sense of fulfilment. Also, others reading the finished piece may have more ease in understanding or identifying with what has been written (overtly, covertly or even ambiguously) if there is a word or line for them to connect with before starting to read. For some poets, a poem without a name is like a car that's missing a wheel. All the other parts of it are there, but it cannot take us or anyone else to the next destination if it is not complete; there is little point in getting into it.

While it may be gratifying for me to see individuals follow my instructions with the intentions that I originally had in mind, I also accept that there should be no limitations to the wordscaper's imagination. Therefore, I would like to emphasize to readers/wordscapers that there are no rights and wrongs in doing these exercises, and you should let your subjective inclinations take the lead where and whenever necessary.

Also, there are no guarantees that these exercises will prove enjoyable or even worthwhile for everyone who tries them. Just as with visual expression involving the use of art materials, we sometimes need to be coaxed into trying something different or that we have not had a positive experience with before. Then, who knows what revelations may follow, and new possibilities open up? (Makin, 1994).

The exercises are each set up under four headings. The first two cover the instructions and examples demonstrating them. The second two refer to some advantages provided by the exercises and offer references for other texts that include similar or related directives. It is advisable to try out the exercises immediately after reading the instructions and examples. The subsequent advantages and references that are included, are not intended to facilitate or detract from the completion of the exercises, but to provide confirmations and comparisons of processes experienced and outcomes achieved, after the poetry has been written.

EXERCISE 1: ALPHABET AND ACROSTIC STARTERS

(1) Instructions

In alphabetical poetry, the first word of each line starts with a different letter of the alphabet. However, since the alphabet is long, and not every letter is easy to start a line with, this exercise favours the shorter acrostic poem. Here, the first letters of each line spell out a word, such as a name, place, food, feeling, or disposition, that is meaningful for the poet.

The lines written, which are started from the individual letters of the chosen word, may involve anywhere from one word to a whole phrase. The chosen word is written vertically (down the page), and the lines stemming from it are written horizontally (across the page). There are two options for the length of the lines written suggested here.

Option One is to write "one word lines."

Option Two is to write "whole phrase lines."

The name of the poem is usually the anagram word itself. However, especially in the case of *Option Two*, a conclusion or focus drawn from the lines created, can be an appropriate alternative.

(2) Examples

(of Option One)

Fear

F	*Feelings*
E	*Energy*
A	*Achievement*
R	*Reborn*

(of Option Two)

Adjusting to Separation

S	*Sad that we can't be together*
O	*Open to trying again*
R	*Restless without you*
R	*Reflective on every level*
Y	*Yearning for you constantly*

(3) Advantages

There is an immediate sense of achievement for the poet who completes this exercise. Very clear conclusions and insights are arrived at quickly, and with a minimum of effort, especially in the poems that are derived from Option One. Subjects that are close to the heart at the time of writing are usually the ones that are touched.

(4) References

Others who have used a variation on this exercise are Arleen McCarty Hynes and Mary Hynes-Berry (1994): "Alphabetical Poetry."

EXERCISE 2: LIST-MAKING THEMES

(1) Instructions

For this poem, there are two options.

Option One is to make a list about a specific subject: person, object, activity, or idea, the possibilities being anywhere from lipstick to daydreaming.

Option Two also involves the making of a list, but this time on a variety of unrelated subjects all listed together: people, objects, activities or ideas.

For Both Options a summative remark is made about the list after it is completed, and the title of the poem focuses on what is referred to in

the list. If the list is made from unrelated items, this is a good opportunity to link them all together under one heading, finding out what
their connection might be.

(2) Examples

(of Option One)

The Sport

Equipment, preparation,
Commitment, concentration, focus
Control, win or lose
Simply playing means winning

(of Option Two)

Lost Love

Old love letters, moist handkerchiefs,
Cold tea, dirty clothes, take-away food containers,
C.D. player blasting, taxi waiting, phone ringing
What are you trying to get over?

(3) Advantages

Making a list is particularly helpful for people who tend to be too
preoccupied with grammar and sentence construction. With only the
ordering of images to ponder, there is less to worry about. In fact, the
poet will be surprised about the ease and speed with which the final
poem is completed.

(4) References

Another person who has used a variation on this exercise is Roger
Mitchell, in Behn and Twichell (1992): "Breaking the Sentence or, No
Sentences but in Things."

EXERCISE 3: COLOUR SELECTIONS

(1) Instructions

The poet should select a colour and then write a number of lines in which its name or properties and feelings attached to it are included. Some universal, symbolic associations to colour are: *red for anger; grey for gloom;* and *yellow for energy.* However, personal symbolic associations may be very different: *red for the cherries that we used to pick every summer; grey for the pond near our house when the sky clouds over,* and *yellow for the bananas in a bowl in my mother's kitchen.* Some may think of less prominent colours also, with which they have a more unique association: for instance, flaming pink, which is worn to be noticed.

Repeating the name of the colour throughout the poem keeps bringing the poet back to the triggering subject and what is more directly associated with it. However, it is not always easy to remember or convenient to do so once one has begun to write and the ideas start flowing unprompted.

Option One is to insist on the repetition of the colour's name.

Option Two is to use the colour's name in the title of the poem, and have the poem itself be about that colour without including more than an initial mention of its name with which to start or end.

Option Three is to make no mention of the colour's name throughout the poem, except in the title.

The tendency for digression will be stronger in the second two options. However, some of the digressions can be equally interesting.

(2) Examples

(of Option One)

Blue

Blue again
Like ice,
Cold, numb,
The pain of blue,
Being blue

Endless skies, blue skies ahead,
No reprieve, no break
For others they lead to positive conclusion,
But for me, blue skies,
Who knows?
Maybe one day soon my time will come
To experience happier sides of life

(of Option Two)

Black

She wears black again
On nails, lips and eyes
Oh why can't she be the child she once was
Alone, cold,
Does not know who she is
Doc. Martin boots and combat too,
Those chains will keep her confined.
Someday soon she will see
that black can have a happier side
and may bring some new color to life.

(of Option Three)

Cream

Clean and fresh
Non-controversial
Always in place
Never jarring
Bright and happy
Contented and peaceful
Elegant and restrained
Idyllic Summer

(3) Advantages

Colour features significantly in all of our lives, even if we take a "black and white" approach. No matter the environment that we live in or how we fill our days, dim lighting or a meadow full of poppies evoke a variety of emotional responses in everyone. There are good associations and bad associations with objects, places and people, and colour may be a significant trigger for any of them: *the old brown oak table, which is a family heirloom; the deep blue sea, where the bad boating accident happened; or Aunt Mildred's emerald green hat, that she made a spectacle of herself wearing.*

The colours that we choose may tell us more about our personalities or what kind of a day we are having than we realise when actually writing these poems. Looking back on them a week or two later, we may understand more clearly the reasons for our choices at the time of writing, what we may really have been going through then. Choices are not usually accidental, when it is the unconscious mind that has made them.

(4) References

Another person who has used a variation on this exercise is Elizabeth Spires in Behn and Twichell (1992): "Writing the Spectrum."

EXERCISE 4: SOMETHING/SOMEONE SIGNIFICANT IDEAS

(1) Instructions

The poet should think about a particular object (every day item) or person in one's life, such as a chair or the baby-sitter, then start to write a list of functions or activities (and behaviours) that give this object or person a recognizable identity—symbolize them. For instance, a chair supports, comforts, holds, fits around a table etc. Once the list has been created, the poem is under way. After the list has been completed, a summative statement is given which indicates a theme or insight connected with the subject or object of the poem. For instance, if the object is *chocolate*, the poet may end by saying: "*So, I eat as much as possible, because it does me good.*"

(2) Examples

(of an object)   **My Organizer**

(list of functions)   *Memory, aging, busy life,*
                            Sheer volume to be retained
                            Recalling sense of achievement instead of
                            Irritation and annoyance
                            Lists of tasks completed
                            Shopping remembered
                            Satisfaction to self and others
                            Dates, birthdays, anniversaries
                            Letters, overdue visits, invitations
(summary statement)   *A reminder of pleasures given*

(of a person)   **Best Friend**

(list of activities)   *Sun block, quarters*
                            Ice cold beer, sugar candy
                            Volley ball and hanging out
                            Big strong arms and Red Sox games
                            Hugs that go on forever
                            Missing my plane, waiting up all night
                            Long-distance phone calls
                            Like a big brother to a little sister
(summary statement)   *Always there for me, I miss him*

(3) Advantages

This exercise was originally devised with inanimate objects in mind, giving them life and voice. However, research volunteers' digressions from the original instruction caused me to broaden its scope. People, it seems, need to talk about people, especially those who are close to them or authority figures, and will always find some way to include them if they can. For some, people and objects hold similar significance. The fortunate family-oriented person may have a familiar loving human face to come home to at nighttime. In contrast, the anxious workaholic may rely on the smooth operation of a highly programmed but sometimes unpredictable computer to have a stress-free weekend.

This exercise clearly points out our needs and priorities, and how dependent or otherwise we may be on elements or aspects of the world around us, what frustrates us and whom we may miss.

(4) References

A person who has used a variation on this exercise is Jack Myers in Behn and Twichell (1992): "The Fill-In-The-Blanks or Definition Poem." Myers also recommends, for variety, its use with abstractions such as "democracy" and collective nouns, such as "American poetry."

EXERCISE 5: THE CINQUAINE-LIKE WAY

(1) Instructions

The poet should follow the instructions set out here. The result will be a ten-word poem with four lines to it, and a name.

Content	Length
Line 1: Title - a noun	1 word
Line 2: Describes the title	2 words
Line 3: Action words or phrases about the title	3 words
Line 4: A feeling about the title	4 words
Line 5: Refers to the title	1 word

(2) Examples

Heat

Warm, comforting
Radiates all around
Chases winter's blues away
Necessary

Compartments *

Independent choices
Time divided fairly
Make more people happy
Peaceful

(3) Advantages

For poets who are anxious about themes and forms that they should use, self-expression can be facilitated by having a clear and concise structure to follow. Then, words and phrases will come up to fit the instructions: these probably would not have been thought of other-wise, or arranged in the particular order requested. Also, for those who are too verbose, the restrictions dictated by the number and type of words limited to each line can be challenging. When the poem is complete, whoever has written it, whether reserved or profuse, will have a justifiable sense of satisfaction from being able to follow a set of simple and strategic directives.

(4) References

Arleen McCarty Hynes and Mary Hynes-Berry (1994) refer to "Cinquaine Poetry" describing it as a form that is related to haiku and tanka. It depends on brevity and the juxtaposition of images, its lines being made up of stresses, syllables, and words. They say that Adelaide Crapsey, the American poet, invented it, and Robert Lubers has used it successfully with both hospitalized and non-hospitalized psychiatric patients. (I have adopted the same format as his in the instructions given here in point (1).

---

* *A note on interpreting this poem:* The poet was referring to the ability to compartmentalize in the brain, and one's life. However, readers may think that her words apply to compartments on a train. Reading another's poems without knowing their context opens the way to various meanings being bestowed on it. The reader usually comes up with the one that is most appropriate to circumstances in their own life at the time of reading, whether it is the meaning intended by the poet or not. The act of doing this is known as projection, and is particularly obvious with viewers reactions to visual art pieces. (Makin, 1994, pp. 34 - 39)

EXERCISE 6: ASSOCIATION-MAKING TECHNIQUES

(1) Instructions

The poet should close his or her eyes and imagine a word. Once a word has come up this can be used as a "key word." The second step is to close one's eyes again, and think of six words that can connect with the "key word." For instance, *blocks* (as a "key word") can be associated with: *no entry, impasses, closed, stifling, uncreative,* and *boring.*

The third step is to write down the key word, putting three of the words just associated with it underneath it, going vertically (down the page), and the other three, along side it, going horizontally (across the page). The fourth step is to focus on each of the three vertical words, then think of four new words that might connect with each of them, writing them across the page.

For the fifth step, when all 16 words have been decided on and written down, there are three options:

Option One is for the poet to take a few moments to reflect on them, how their order might be rearranged, with new words (like conjunctions: *and, but, because;* and prepositions: *on, into, under*) being added, and whichever of the original 16 words that don't seem to fit being excluded. Finally, a poem will start to emerge that the poet can rework until it feels complete.

Option Two is not to add or take away any words. The poem may feel complete to the poet just the way it is.

Option Three is for the poet to decide to use only the occasional word (if at all) that has been connected with the key word, concentrating on messages and insights that spring to mind from them instead. Then, they may write a fresh poem that relates to or affirms that new knowledge gained.

(2) Examples

(of option one)

key word: DETERMINED	resolute, unflinching, believing
Concentrating	strength, substance, healing
Thoughtful	considerate, with feelings, kind
Tenacious	persistent, cohesive, afloat

Determined

When life's platform disappears
Be determined to stay afloat
Use your strength, concentrate, be cohesive
Believe in yourself, your thoughts, your feelings
Tenacity is a way of healing

(Of Option Two)

key word: TIME	clock, good happy youth, loss
Late	annoyance, incomplete, dissatisfied
Thief	anger, disbelief, distressing
Death	finality, too late, another time

Time Clock

Time clock, good happy youth, loss
Late, annoyance, incomplete, dissatisfied
Thief, anger, disbelief, distressing
Death, finality, too late, another time

(of Option Three)
also from the "key word" TIME)

The Wisdom of Age

Youthful energy, good and happy times
Clock moving fast, never enough time

Annoyance and loss, missed opportunities,
Broken friendships

Dissatisfaction, unfinished business,
Uncompleted tasks

Anger, disbelief, reliving,
Hoping for a different ending

Finality—too late
Adjustment, rebirth, moving on

Improvement, optimism, hope, and maybe satisfaction
Next time

(3) Advantages

Our unconscious may be sending us a message in the "free associa-tions" that it projects into our consciousness. Even though we might not consciously understand why very different words have come up next to each other, when we explore further, a connection may become apparent.

(4) References

Another person who has used a variation on this exercise is Carol Muske in Behn and Twichell (1992): "Translations: Idea to Image."

Chapter 2
POETICALLY WISE RESOURCES

The National Association for Poetry Therapy

In the late 1960s, while Jack Leedy continued Eli Greifer's work, exploring poetry's therapeutic benefits in psychiatry (as referred to in Part One of this book), two others were busy in related pursuits. In the Nassau County Recreation Department, Ann White was working on creating an experimental project to bring the therapeutic benefits of poetry into hospitals, rehabilitation centres, and schools for special children. And at the Institute for Sociotherapy in New York, Gil Schloss was conducting "psychopoetry" sessions with individuals and groups. In 1969, the three joined with others to found the Association for Poetry Therapy. Morris R. Morrison, who was a poet and educator and great supporter of the association drafted the first systematic set of standards for certification in the field.

In 1980, the A.P.T. became the N.A.P.T., a national non-profit association. The N.A.P.T. is the "official membership organization representing poetry therapists." According to its Guide (1993), its role is to provide information and publications as well as sponsoring a national conference, supporting education, research and training, and representing the field to other organizations, practitioners, and the general public.

The National Association for Poetry Therapy's 18th Annual Conference, "Creating Connection to Self, Community, and Environment" which was held in April-May 1998 in San José, attracted 164 participants. The membership of the Association at the time of the conference totaled approximately 389, with 20 being "foreign subscribers" (of which I am one). There are currently 23 active Certified Poetry Therapists (C.P.T.s) and 22 active Registered Poetry Therapists (R.P.T.s). Approximately forty others have let their annual activation fee lapse (as happens in other professional organizations); a significant number of whom may still be using their designation. There are also ten "mentor supervisors" who are actively involved with trainees and in training programs.

Poetry Therapy Training Standards

From the 1970s onwards, a number of poetry therapy training programs and groups began to emerge across the United States. The most notable and comprehensive of which was started in 1974 at St. Elizabeths Hospital in Washington D.C. by Arleen Hynes, a librarian at the hospital, and psychiatrist, Kenneth Gorelick. In California, The Poetry Therapy Institute was developed by Arthur Lerner; in Austin Texas, Morris R. Morrison founded the American Academy of Poetry Therapy; and in Columbus, Ohio, Jennifer Bosveld created the Ohio Poetry Therapy Center and Library

The different poetry therapy training programs that were developed in the 1970s were each, originally, responsible for creating and devising their own certificates (and standards). Then, in the 1980s, with the evolution of the A.P.T. into the N.A.P.T., uniform requirements were established and enforced by a Credentials Committee. Today, though thousands of professionals use poetry and various forms of literature to help promote personal growth and achieve therapeutic goals with clients, as mentioned in the introduction to this book, the only persons officially authorized to call themselves *poetry therapists* in the United States, are those who have successfully completed the training requirements of the N.A.P.T.

Reading On

This book sets out to consider the concept of poetry as healer and friend in as comprehensive a way as possible, to appeal to readers of all backgrounds and levels of interest. In so doing, however, I am well aware of its potential limitations for some. For readers who are more acquainted with some of the subjects covered and have specific interests and needs, there may not be enough relevant details given pertaining to those. Also, for readers who were previously unfamiliar with or who had limited knowledge in this area, maybe their appetites will be wetted to know of more resources.

Therefore, as this book draws to a close, I have decided to offer some recommendations for further reading. The only category that I am not giving suggestions for here is poetry books and anthologies. It would be simple for me to list the "classics" (and I have already cited others who have done so in Part One of this book), and beyond the classics, the taste, purpose, and previous background of the reader should influence the selections made. As the popularity of poetry grows, most of the larger bookstores carry substantial sections of contemporary poetry. Readers should take their time browsing through these, finding out which appeal to their emotional, spiritual, and situational yearnings: an author that either says, "I've been there too," or one who takes them off to another place, very different from the one in which they are.

It is also important to note that the lists included here are not exhaustive, and there are many more fine resources available on tape and in magazines, as well as in book form. I have chosen to focus on books that were initially helpful to me personally, and latterly, for the purposes of preparing this book.

(1) Poetry Therapy

Harrower, Molly. *The Therapy of Poetry*. New Jersey: Jason Aronson Inc., 1995

Leedy, Jack, J. (ed.). *Poetry as Healer. Mending The Troubled Mind.* New York: Vanguard Press, 1985

Lerner, Arthur (ed.). *Poetry in the Therapeutic Experience*. St. Louis, MO.: M.M.B. Music Inc., 1994

Lerner, A. and Mahlendorf, U.R. (eds.). *Life Guidance Through Literature.* Chicago: The American Library Association, 1992

McCarty Hynes, Arleen. and Hynes-Berry, Mary. *Biblio/Poetry Therapy. The Interactive Process. A Handbook.* St. Cloud, MN.: North Star Press, 1994

Morrison, Morris R. (ed.). *Poetry as Therapy*. New York: Human Sciences Press, 1987

(2) Stimulation For Original/Creative Writing

Adams, Kathleen. *Journal to the Self. Twenty-Two Paths to Personal Growth*. New York: Warner Books, 1990

Cameron, Julia. *The Artist's Way*. New York: Jeremy P. Tarcher, 1992

Goldberg, Bonni. *Room to Write. Daily Invitations to a Writer's Life.* New York: Jeremy P. Tarcher, 1996

Goldberg, Natalie. *Writing Down the Bones. Freeing the Writer Within.* Boston: Shambhala, 1986

(3) With Poetry Writing Exercises

Behn, Robin. and Twichell, Chase. (eds.). *The Practice of Poetry. Writing Exercises from Poets Who Teach.* New York: Harper Perennial, 1992

Bosveld, Jennifer. *Topics For Getting In Touch. A Poetry Therapy Sourcebook* (34th Printing). Ohio: Pudding House Publications, 1995

Fox, John. *Finding What You Didn't Lose. Expressing Your Truth and Creativity Through Poem-Making.* New York: Tarcher/Putnam, 1995

(4) Product-Oriented Poetry

Raffel, Burton. *How to Read A Poem.* New York: Meridian, 1984

Deutsch, Babette. *Poetry Handbook. A Dictionary of Terms.* (Fourth Edition). New York: Harper Perennial, 1974

Greer, Germaine. *Slip-Shod Sibyls. Recognition, Rejection and the Woman Poet.* London, U.K: Viking, 1995

Kowit, Steve. *In the Palm of Your Hand. The Poet's Portable Workshop.* Maine: Tilbury House, 1995

(5) Poetry and Personal Writing for Children

Capacchione, Lucia. *The Creative Journal for Children. A Guide for Parents, Teachers and Counselors.* Boston: Shambhala, 1989

Koch, Kenneth. *Wishes, Lies, and Dreams. Teaching Children to Write Poetry.* New York: Harper and Row, 1970

(6) Individual and Social Concerns

André, Rae. *Positive Solitude. A Practical Program for Mastering Loneliness and Achieving Self-Fulfillment.* New York: Harper Perennial, 1992

Bly, Robert., Hillman, James. and Meade, Michael (eds.). *The Rag and Bone Shop of the Heart. Poems for Men.* New York: Harper Perennial, 1993

Field, Joanna. *A Life of One's Own.* New York: Tarcher Putnam, 1981

Frankl, Viktor E. *Man's Search For Meaning. Revised and Updated.* New York, London: Washington Square Press, A Division of Simon & Schuster Inc., 1984

Goleman, Daniel. *Emotional Intelligence. Why It Can Matter More Than I.Q.* New York: Bantam Books, 1995

Roland, Alan. *In Search of Self in India and Japan. Toward a Cross-Cultural Psychology.*
  New Jersey: Princeton University Press, 1989
Rutter, Michael. and Marjorie. *Developing Minds. Challenge and Continuity Across the
  Life Span.* London: Penguin Books, 1993
Storr, Anthony. *The Integrity of the Personality.* New York: Ballantine Books, 1992

CONCLUSION

Poetry is the rearing in language of a desire whose end lies beyond language.
Tom Lilburn, 1995

Dinora Pines (1993) was first a linguist and then a general practitioner and dermatologist, respectively, before her training as a psychoanalyst. So, for her, "Sensitive listening to language, the choice of words and their meaning, is as important in psychoanalysis as in literature." For me, wordscaping opportunities are primary promoters of that sensitive listening to language: the words that are chosen spontaneously and arranged in poetic formats can convey meanings that are a lot more potent than they would be in prose or in regular conversation.

The honesty and accuracy of my spontaneously written wordscapes astounds me. It leaves a clear record of feelings and reflections expressed concisely. Even when I have been in denial, these wordscapes have not aided concealment, and have given me powerful cautionary messages. According to Irvin Yalom (1989): "The first step in all therapeutic change is responsibility assumption. If one feels in no way responsible for one's predicament, how can one change it?" When I read back over the wordscapes chosen for inclusion in this collection, I am able to accept that any intensity that I felt was not only in my imagination, and note that positive feelings (although more limited) are described just as vigourously as the painful ones.

Also, at points in time, I realise that it has been hard for me to come to terms with the loss of the beautiful feelings that my wordscaping has been able to capture, and to acknowledge that although I was able to have them, their perpetuation was not possible. Shaun McNiff (1981) stated, "Spontaneous poetry is often written in anger as a form of protest, as an expression of longing or loss, and as an affirmation of the self in the face of stressful situations."

209

In the popular movie, "Shadowlands," C.S. Lewis (played by Anthony Hopkins) stated that man reads to know that he is not alone. The spontaneously written wordscapes included in this book reveal the basic traits, needs and desires that we all share. It is hard to grow up, and then, if we feel that we have got there, maintain ourselves, and endeavour to realise long-held hopes and dreams.

Sadness is the emotion that none of us like to have, but the one that helps us to grow, as is confirmed by numerous commentators. Thanks to sadness some of the world's greatest poets have realised their creative and artistic potentials. With respect to myself, I am sure that many of my wordscaping urges would never have been realised to the same degree or with the same profundity if I had not undergone the extreme discomforts of deep and all-pervading sadnesses. Kay Redfield Jamison (1994) states, "Learning through intense, extreme, and often painful experiences, and using what has been learned to add meaning and depth to creative work, is probably the most widely accepted and written about aspect of the relationship between melancholy, madness and the artistic experience."

It is with passion and from passion that the spontaneous wordscapes included in this book are fueled; and with compassion and from compassion that the narrative texts are composed and organized. According to Viktor Frankl (1984), "The way in which a man accepts his fate and all the suffering it entails, the way in which he takes up his cross, gives him ample opportunity—even under the most difficult circumstances—to add a deeper meaning to his life." Hopefully, the utilization of wordscaping or poetry as therapy, as shown by some of the techniques and ideas suggested in this book, will prove helpful to others in there own endeavours and explorations.

There is no doubt that poetry is wise. The key to its wisdom is found in its simplicity. Wordscaping encourages personal revelations by poets which say, "I've been there too." Being able to put personal revelations into words is not only empowering for the wordscapes, but the reader/listener too; universal identification and understanding being a catalyst for public healing and growth.

BIBLIOGRAPHY

Adams, Kathleen. *Journal to the Self. Twenty-Two Paths to Personal Growth.* New York: Warner Books, 1990.

André, Rae. *Positive Solitude. A Practical Program for Mastering Loneliness and Achieving Self-Fulfillment.* New York: Harper Perennial, 1992

Barrett, Carol. "Why Write? Confessions Of a Poet" *The Network.* (A Union Institute Publication) 13/2 (1996): 33 - 35.

Bean, Manya. "The Poetry of Countertransference." *The Arts in Psychotherapy. 19* (1992): 347 - 358.

Behn, Robin. & Twichell, Chase. (eds.). *The Practice of Poetry. Writing Exercises from Poets Who Teach.* New York: Harper Perennial, 1992.

Bly, Robert. *A Little Book on the Human Shadow.* San Francisco: Harper, 1988.

Bly, Robert. *Into The Deep: Male Mysteries.* Colorado: Sounds True Recordings, 1991.

Bly, Robert., Hillman, James. & Meade, Michael. (eds.). *The Rag and Bone Shop of the Heart. Poems for Men.* New York: Harper Perennial, 1993.

Bogdan, Robert C. & Knopp Biklen, Sari. *Qualitative Research for Education: An Introduction to Theory and Methods.* Boston: Allyn & Bacon, Inc., 1982

Bosveld, Jennifer. *Topics For Getting In Touch. A Poetry Therapy Sourcebook* (34th Printing). Ohio: Pudding House Publications, 1995.

Bowman, Daniel O. & Halfacre, David L., "Poetry Therapy with the Sexually Abused Adolescent. A Case Study." *The Arts in Psychotherapy.* 21/1 (1994): 11-16.

Briggs, John. & Monaco, Richard. Metaphor: *The Logic of Poetry. A Handbook.* New York: Pace University Press, 1990.

Bringhurst, Robert. "Everywhere Being is Dancing, Knowing is Known." In Tim Lilburn (ed.), *Poetry and Knowing. Speculative Essays and Interviews.* Ontario, Canada: Quarry Press, 1995: 52-64

Cameron, Julia. *The Artist's Way. Part One. Meeting Your Creative Myths and Monsters.* Colorado: Sounds True Recordings, 1993.

Cattaneo, Mariagnese. "Addressing Culture and Values in the Training of Art Therapists." *Art Therapy. Journal of the American Art Therapy Association. 3* (1994): 184-190.

Craib, Ian. *The Importance of Disappointment.* London: Routledge, 1994.

Denzin, Norman K. & Lincoln, Yvonna S. (eds.). *Handbook of Qualitative Research.* California: Sage, 1994.

Deutsch, Babette. *Poetry Handbook. A Dictionary of Terms. Fourth Edition.* New York: Harper Perennial, 1974.

Field, Joanna. *A Life of One's Own.* New York: Tarcher Putnam, 1981.

Fields, Dan. "Poetry on P.B.S." *New Age Journal.* July/August (1995): 58.

Fox, John. *Finding What You Didn't Lose. Expressing Your Truth and Creativity Through Poem-Making* New York: Tarcher/Putnam, 1995.

Frankl, Viktor E. *Man's Search For Meaning.* Revised and Updated. New York, London: Washington Square Press, A Division of Simon & Schuster Inc., 1984.

Gardner, Howard. *Frames of Mind. The Theory of Multiple Intelligences.* New York: Basic Books, 1993.

Gendler, Ruth, J. *The Book of Qualities.* New York: Harper Perennial, 1988.

Goldberg, Bonni. *Room to Write. Daily Invitations to a Writer's Life.* New York: Jeremy P. Tarcher, 1996.

Goldberg, Natalie. *Writing Down the Bones. Freeing the Writer Within.* Boston: Shambhala, 1986.

Goldberg, Natalie. *Writing The Landscape of Your Mind.* Natalie's Minnesota Workshop. St. Austin, Texas: Writer's Audio Shop, 1993.

Goleman, Daniel. *Emotional Intelligence. Why It Can Matter More Than I.Q.* New York: Bantam Books, 1995.

Goodrich-Dunn, Barbara. *"Emptying the Hands." Common Boundary* November/December (1994): 30 - 32.

Greer, Germaine. *Slip-Shod Sibyls. Recognition, Rejection and the Woman Poet.* London, U.K: Viking, 1995.

Harrower, Molly. *The Therapy of Poetry.* New Jersey: Jason Aronson Inc., 1995.

Heller, Peggy. "Biblio/Poetry therapy in the Treatment of Multiple Personality Disorder," *Treating Abuse Today.* 3/4 (1994): 10-15.

Heller, Peggy. "Poetry Therapy Training Manual for Mental Health Professionals." Ph. D. Dissertation, Pacific Western University, 1995.

Heninger, Owen E. "Poetry Therapy in Private Practice. An Odyssey into the Healing Power of Poetry. In Arthur Lerner (ed.), *Poetry in the Therapeutic Experience.* (pp. 57 - 63). St. Louis, MO.: M.M.B. Music Inc., 1994.

Heninger, Owen E. "Poetic Medicine," *Journal of Poetry Therapy.* 8/1 (1994): 21 - 26.

Honton, Margaret. (ed.). *To Go Too Far. The Poet's Job. 73 Poets Show How They Succeeded.* Ohio: Pudding House Publications, 1995.

Jung, Carl G. *Man and His Symbols.* New York: Dell Publishing, 1964.

Knapp, Caroline. *Alice K.'s Guide to Life. One Woman's Quest for Survival, Sanity, and the Perfect New Shoes.* New York: Plume/Penguin, 1994.

Knights, Ben. *The Listening Reader: Fiction and Poetry for Counsellors and Psychotherapists.* London: Jessica Kingsley, 1995.

Knill, Paolo J. "Multiplicity as a Tradition: Theories for Interdisciplinary Arts Therapies—An Overview." *The Arts in Psychotherapy.* 21/5 (1994): 319 - 328.

Koch, Kenneth. Wishes, Lies, and Dreams. Teaching Children to Write Poetry. New York: Harper & Row, 1970.

Kowit, Steve. *In the Palm of Your Hand. The Poet's Portable Workshop.* Maine: Tilbury House, 1995

Leedy, Jack, J. (ed.). *Poetry as Healer. Mending The Troubled Mind.* New York: Vanguard Press, 1985.

Lerner, Arthur (ed.). *Poetry in the Therapeutic Experience.* St. Louis, MO.: M.M.B. Music Inc., 1994.

Lerner, Arthur. "Poetry Therapy Corner," *Journal of Poetry Therapy.* 8/1 (1994): 29 - 33.

Lerner, Arthur. "Poetry Therapy Corner," *Journal of Poetry Therapy.* 9/1 (1995): 47 - 49.

Lerner, Arthur. "Poetry Therapy Corner," *Journal of Poetry Therapy.* 9/2 (1995): 93 - 101.

Lerner, A. & Mahlendorf, U.R. (eds.) *Life Guidance Through Literature.* Chicago: The American Library Association, 1992.

Lester, David. & Terry, Rina. "The Use of Poetry Therapy: Lessons From The Life of Anne Sexton." *The Arts in Psychotherapy.* 19 (1992): 47 - 52.

Lilburn, Tim. (ed.). *Poetry and Knowing. Speculative Essays and Interviews.* Ontario, Canada: Quarry Press Inc., 1995.

Lippin, Richard A., "Poetry and Poetry Therapy: A Conversation with Arthur Lerner. *The Arts in Psychotherapy.* 9 (1982): 167 - 174.

Makin, Susan R. "Fed Up." In *Read,* June 24 - 28 (1968). Hertfordshire, England: Everyweek Educational Press Ltd.: 7.

Makin, Susan R. *A Consumer's Guide to Art Therapy: For Prospective Employers, Clients and Students.* Springfield, IL.: Charles C Thomas, 1994.

Maltman, Kim. "Before the Onset of Modernism." In Tom Lilburn (ed.), *Poetry and Knowing. Speculative Essays and Interviews.* Ontario, Canada: Quarry Press Inc., 1995: 132-148

Mathis, Cleopatra. "An Emotional Landscape for a Group." In Robin Behn & Chase Twichell (eds.), *The Practice of Poetry. Writing Exercises from Poets Who Teach.* (pp. 22 - 26) New York: Harper Perennial, 1992: 22-26

May, Rollo. *The Courage to Create.* New York: W.W. Norton and Company, 1975.

May, Rollo. "Short Takes 1967 - 1992." *Psychology Today.* December (1992): 63.

McCarty Hynes, Arleen. & Hynes-Berry, Mary. *Biblio/Poetry Therapy. The Interactive Process. A Handbook.* St. Cloud, MN.: North Star Press, 1994.

McNiff, Shaun. *The Arts and Psychotherapy.* Springfield, IL.: Charles C Thomas, 1981.

Michaels, Anne. "Cleopatra's Love." In Tom Lilburn (ed.), *Poetry and Knowing. Speculative Essays and Interviews.* Ontario, Canada: Quarry Press Inc., 1995: 177-183

Mitchell, Roger. "Breaking the Sentence; or, No Sentences but in Things." In Robin Behn & Chase Twichell (eds.), *The Practice of Poetry. Writing Exercises from Poets Who Teach.* New York: Harper Perennial, 1992. 37-39

Moore, Thomas. *On Creativity.* Colorado: Sounds True Recordings, 1993.

Moore, Thomas. *Care of the Soul.* New York: Harper Perennial, 1994.

Moore, Thomas. *The Re-Enchantment of Everyday Life.* Harper Perennial: New York, 1996.

Morrison, Morris R. (ed.), *Poetry as Therapy.* New York: Human Sciences Press, 1987.

Moustakas, Clark. *Heuristic Research.* California: Sage, 1990.

Myers, Jack. "The Fill-In-The-Blanks or Definition Poem." In Robin Behn & Chase Twichell (eds.), *The Practice of Poetry. Writing Exercises from Poets Who Teach.* New York: Harper Perennial, 1992: 141-142

National Association for Poetry Therapy, "Guide to Training Requirements For Credentialing as a Poetry Therapist,"1993.

National Association For Poetry Therapy Advisory Committee, "Poetry Therapy Testimony," 1995.

Norwood, Robin. *Why Me, Why This, Why Now. A Guide to Answering Life's Toughest Questions.* Toronto: McClelland & Stewart Inc., 1994.

Nowinski, Joseph. *Hungry Hearts. On Men, Intimacy, Self-Esteem, and Addiction.* New York: Lexington Books, 1993.

Ogden Nash., Selected Poetry of. With an introduction by Archibald MacLeish. New York: Black Dog & Leventhal, 1995.

Patton, Michael Quinn. *Qualitative Evaluation And Research Methods.* Second Edition. California: Sage Publications, 1990.

Perl, Sondra. "Teaching and Practice. Composing Texts, Composing Lives." *Harvard Educational Review. 64/4* (1994): 427 - 449.

Philipson, Ilene J. *On the Shoulders of Women. The Feminization of Psychotherapy.* New York: The Guilford Press, 1993.

Pines, Dinora. *A Woman's Unconscious Use of Her Body. A Psychoanalytical Perspective.* London: Virago Press, 1993.

Pinkola Estes, Clarissa. *The Creative Fire. Myths and Stories about the Cycles of Creativity.* Colorado: Sounds True Recordings, 1991.

Pinsky, Robert. *Poetry and the World.* New York: The Ecco Press, 1988.

Poe. Poems and Prose. Everyman's Library Pocket Poets. New York, Toronto: Alfred A. Knopf, 1995.

Progoff, Ira. *At A Journal Workshop.* New York: Tarcher/Putnam, 1992.

Raffel, Burton. *How to Read A Poem.* New York: Meridian, 1984.

Redfield Jamison, Kay. *Touched With Fire. Manic Depressive Illness and the Artistic Temperament.* New York: The Free Press, 1994.

Redfield Jamison, Kay. *An Unquiet Mind. A Memoir of Moods and Madness.* New York: Alfred A. Knopf, 1995.

Rodenhauser, Paul. "Unlocking Creativity: Connections Between Psychic and External Reality," *Journal of Poetry Therapy.* 8/1 (1994): 15 - 19.

Roland, Alan. *In Search of Self in India and Japan . Toward a Cross-Cultural Psychology.* New Jersey: Princeton University Press, 1989.

Rossiter, Charles. "Contemporary Multicultural North American Poetry and Poetry Therapy. *Journal of Poetry Therapy.* 8/4 (1994): 191 - 194.

Rutter, Michael. & Rutter, Marjorie. *Developing Minds. Challenge and Continuity Across the Life Span.* London, Penguin Books, 1993.

Schloss, Gilbert A., & Grundy, Dominick E. "Action Techniques in Psychotherapy." In Arthur Lerner (ed.), *Poetry in the Therapeutic Experience.* St. Louis, MO.: M.M.B. Music Inc., 1994: 81-95

Shotter, John. *Cultural Politics of Everyday Life.* Toronto: University of Toronto Press, 1993.

Singer, June. *The Sadness of the Successful Woman. Archetypal Roots of Female Depression.* Colorado: Sounds True Recordings, 1993.

Solari, Rose. "The Sound of What Matters." *Common Boundary.* January/February (1996): 24 - 32.

Spires, Elizabeth. "Writing the Spectrum." In Robin Behn & Chase Twichell (eds.), *The Practice of Poetry. Writing Exercises from Poets Who Teach.* New York: Harper Perennial, 1992: 54-55

Stafford, William. *Passwords.* New York: Harper Perennial, 1991: xiii.

Steffler, John. "Language as Matter." In Tim Lilburn (ed.), *Poetry and Knowing. Speculative Essays and Interviews.* Ontario, Canada: Quarry Press, 1995: 45-51

Stewart, Donna E. & Stotland, Nada L. (eds.). *Psychological Aspects of Women's Health Care.* Washington D.C.: American Psychiatric Press Inc., 1993.

Storr, Anthony. *Churchill's Black Dog, Kafka's Mice and Other Phenomena of the Human Mind.* New York, Ballantine Books, 1988.

Storr, Anthony. *Solitude. A Return to the Self.* New York: Ballantine Books, 1988.

Storr, Anthony. *The Integrity of the Personality.* New York: Ballantine Books, 1992.

Storr, Anthony. *The Dynamics of Creation.* London: Penguin Books, 1972.

Strauss, Anselm. & Corbin, Juliet. *Basics of Qualitative Research. Grounded Theory, Procedures and Techniques.* Sage, 1990.

Strean, Herbert S. *Psychotherapy with the Unattached.* New Jersey: Jason Aronson Inc., 1995.

Turner, Barbara F. & Troll, Lillian E. (eds.). *Women Growing Older. Psychological Perspectives.* Thousand Oaks, California: Sage Publications, 1994.

Wakefield, Dan. "The Joy of Creation." *Common Boundary.* January/February: (1995): 72.

Waldman, Anne. "Intriguing Objects Exercise." In Robin Behn and Chase Twichell (eds.), *The Practice of Poetry. Writing Exercises from Poets Who Teach.* New York: Harper Perennial, 1992: 35-36

Walker, Alice., Allende, Isabel, & Bolen, Jean Shinoda. *Giving Birth, Finding Form. Three Writers Explore Their Lives, Their Loves, Their Art.* Colorado: Sounds True Recordings, 1993

Wallace, Edith. "Introduction to a Poet." *The Arts in Psychotherapy.* 9 (1982): 175 - 176.

Waters, Michael. "Auction First Lines." In Robin Behn.& Chase Twichell (eds.), *The Practice of Poetry. Writing Exercises from Poets Who Teach.* New York: Harper Perennial, 1992: 15-16

Webb, Wilse, B. "A Dream Is A Poem: A Metaphorical Analysis." *Dreaming.* 2/3 (1992): 191 - 201.

Wente, Margaret. "The Thinking Woman's Heartthrob." in *The Globe and Mail,* Toronto (1994): Saturday February 12, A 2.

Woodman, Marion. *Holding the Tension of the Opposites. A Jungian analyst examines the divine tension that arises when we achieve integration with our shadow sides.* Colorado: Sounds True Recordings, 1991.

Yalom, Irvin D. *Love's Executioner & Other Tales of Psychotherapy.* New York: Harper Perennial, 1989.

AUTHOR INDEX

Akhmatova, A., 24

Barrett, C., 27, 28
Beddoes, T. L., 33
Bell, G., 37
Berger, A., 37
Blake, W., 24, 33
Bly, R., 11, 12, 13, 24–26, 101, 135, 165, 168
Bosveld, J., 205
Briggs, J., 3, 6
Bringhurst, R., 20, 21
Burton, R., 19, 20
Byron, G. G. (Lord), 33

Cane, M., 44
Chatterton, T., 33
Church, P. P., 49
Clare, J., 33
Cohen, L., 54
Coleridge, H., 33
Coleridge, S. T., 33
Cousins, N., 42
Cowper, W., 33
Craib, I., 13, 105, 124
Crapsey, A., 200
Crothers, S., 36

Daley, G., 33
Deutsch, B., 19

Eady, C., 15

Fergusson, R., 33
Fields, D., 15
Forché, C., 18
Fox, J., 55
Frankl, V., 11, 58, 210

Gardner, H., 24, 139

Goleman, D., 94, 104, 111, 117, 124, 129, 134, 135, 151, 174, 178, 189
Goodrich-Dunn, B., 18
Gorelick, K., 205
Graves, R., 42, 143
Greene, G., 24
Greer, G., 3, 24, 27, 29, 51, 52
Greifer, E., 37, 204
Guilford, J. P., 190

Hale, S. J., 29
Harrower, M., 22, 23, 41, 43–45, 52, 53, 58, 165
Heller, P., 39–41
Henninger, O. E., 31
Hynes, A. M., 193, 200, 205
Hynes-Berry, M., 193, 200

Ignatow, D., 24

Jamison, K. R., 24, 27, 31, 33, 52, 166, 171–73, 190, 210

Knapp, C., 159
Knight, E., 24
Knights, B., 67
Kramer, A., 37

Laux, D., 51
Lawrence, D. H., 24
Leedy, J., 35, 37, 42, 204
Lerner, A., 16, 17, 26, 42, 55, 187, 190, 205
Lester, D., 28, 29
Lewis, C. S., 210
Lilburn, T., 209
Lippin, R., 27, 55
Lubers, R., 200

Mahlendodrf, U., 41

217

SUBJECT INDEX

219

POETIC TOPICS INDEX